Chris Rock

COMEDIAN AND ACTOR

Black Americans of Achievement

LEGACY EDITION

Muhammad Ali

Maya Angelou

Josephine Baker

Johnnie Cochran

Frederick Douglass

W.E.B. Du Bois

Marcus Garvey

Savion Glover

Alex Haley

Jimi Hendrix

Langston Hughes

Jesse Jackson

Scott Joplin

Coretta Scott King

Martin Luther King, Jr.

Malcolm X

Bob Marley

Thurgood Marshall

Jesse Owens

Rosa Parks

Colin Powell

Chris Rock

Sojourner Truth

Harriet Tubman

Nat Turner

Booker T. Washington

Oprah Winfrey

Black Americans of Achievement
LEGACY EDITION

Chris Rock

COMEDIAN AND ACTOR

Anne M. Todd

CHELSEA HOUSE
PUBLISHERS
An imprint of Infobase Publishing

Chris Rock

Chelsea House
An imprint of Infobase Publishing
132 West 31st Street
New York NY 10001

ISBN-13: 978-0-7910-9225-5

Library of Congress Cataloging-in-Publication Data
Todd, Anne M.
  Chris Rock / Anne Todd.
    p. cm. — (Black Americans of achievement, legacy edition)
  Includes bibliographical references and index.
  ISBN 0-7910-9225-9 (hardcover)
  1. Rock, Chris. 2. Comedians—United States—Biography. 3. African American comedians—United States—Biography. I. Title. II. Series.
  PN2287.R717T63 2006
  792.702'8092—dc22   2006007332

Chelsea House books are available at special discounts when purchased in bulk quantities for businesses, associations, institutions, or sales promotions. Please call our Special Sales Department in New York at (212) 967-8800 or (800) 322-8755.

You can find Chelsea House on the World Wide Web at http://www.chelseahouse.com

Series and cover design by Takeshi Takahashi

Printed in the United States of America

Bang FOF 10 9 8 7 6 5 4 3 2

This book is printed on acid-free paper.

All links and web addresses were checked and verified to be correct at the time of publication. Because of the dynamic nature of the web, some addresses and links may have changed since publication and may no longer be valid.

Contents

No Pain, No Gain

Only the backstage area of a theater is visible. An announcer yells, "Live, from the Takoma Theatre in Washington, D.C.... Are ... you ... ready? ... It's Chri-i-i-s R-o-o-o-c-k!" The crowd cheers in anticipation of the comedian's entrance. The camera closes in on a battered, red door with the name "Chris Rock" printed on a small card. The camera slowly pans down the length of the door to the floor. The door opens and there is a glimpse of an all-black outfit—shirt, pants, belt, and shiny leather jacket—as a person emerges from the dressing room. The only items of clothing that are not all black are the shoes, which are glossy white on top. As the person walks through the doorway, the camera remains on his shoes. The shoes proceed through a dark, narrow passageway leading to the main stage, and the audience's excitement level builds. The shoes pass by unused lockers, step over cables and other wiring, and make their way through miscellaneous theater equipment.

Meanwhile, images showing the covers of comedy albums starring other comedians appear on screen and then fade away. They include the greats: Bill Cosby, Dick Gregory, Flip Wilson (as the character Geraldine), Richard Pryor, Steve Martin, Pigmeat Markham, Woody Allen, and Eddie Murphy. These are the people who inspired Chris Rock to become a comedian. Rock spent hours and hours of his childhood listening to these comedy albums—he used to recite parts of them to his family and friends; now Rock was about to star in his own comedy special.

Suddenly, Chris Rock is striding onto the stage as spotlights fill the theater with light. The crowd goes wild. Long panels of gold and silver curtains drape across the back and sides of the stage. An enormous, bright blue "CR" statue is sitting on a raised platform backstage in the center. Each letter is outlined in silver.

Rock smiles and greets the audience, welcoming the cheers and applause with outstretched arms. He looks into the crowd with sharp, alert, smiling eyes. He is all style and stage presence. He's young, he's hip, and he's in the moment. He carries his thin body and average height with pride and confidence. The audience can sense the energy radiating from him. The spotlight follows his long strides back and forth across the stage as he begins his monologue. He relays keen observations about politics, relationships, racism, and show business. His voice and presence permeate the theater. Sometimes he stops in his tracks and looks at the audience as if to say, "Can you *believe* that?" All the while, the theater fills with laughter. Rock's confident demeanor and energetic performance capture the attention of every person in the audience. He owns the stage—he controls the crowd.

A PIVOTAL SHOW

Many critics consider this HBO special from 1996, *Chris Rock: Bring the Pain,* to be the turning point in Rock's career.

Backstage at the 49th Annual Primetime Emmy Awards, Chris Rock joked around, holding the two Emmys he won for his comedy special, *Chris Rock: Bring the Pain*. The awards were for outstanding writing for a variety or music program and outstanding variety, music, or comedy special. *Bring the Pain* launched Rock's career to the next level.

It brought Rock the fame and recognition he had previously lacked. Before *Bring the Pain*, Rock spent his time performing in comedy clubs and at colleges around the United States. Although he was getting gigs, he wasn't making headlines and he wasn't drawing big audiences. He had not broken into the major comedy scene. People did recognize Rock from his stint on the popular television show *Saturday Night Live*. His work on that show, though, was thought to be sloppy by some and underdeveloped by others. So, although *Saturday Night Live* itself was a big success, Rock was still relatively unknown. When HBO invited him to perform in a comedy special, Rock accepted.

Rock had worked hard over the previous year to perfect his comedy and improve his stage presence. He wanted to highlight these improvements in *Bring the Pain.* Shortly before taping the special, he bumped into a fellow comedian, Andrew Dice Clay. Clay reminded Rock that this could be Rock's big break; Clay advised Rock to take the special seriously. He also suggested that Rock should watch the *Rocky* movies (about boxer Rocky Balboa) to help him get in the right frame of mind for the project. Like a boxer, Rock needed to train for his big day. Viewing the movies helped him. Chris Rock focused on what needed to get done and did it. He worked at comedy clubs right up until his big special. He fine-tuned the comedy that worked and took out or revised what did not. Rock was left with good material—intelligent, honest, and witty, characteristics that would come to define his comedy in the years to come.

Rock's dedication and determination paid off. *Bring the Pain* was a huge success. He had connected with people about everyday issues. The comedy special brought Rock offers to appear in several big-name movies and television programs. *Entertainment Weekly* and *Time* magazines would later call Rock the "funniest man in America." After *Bring the Pain,* critics and fans began to compare Rock with some of his own idols, Richard Pryor and Eddie Murphy. Rock's career jumped to a new level—he may have been a good comedian before *Bring the Pain,* but now he was on his way to becoming a great one.

2

Childhood

On Sunday evening, February 7, 1965, three weeks before her due date, Rose Rock gave birth to her first son, Chris, at Georgetown Memorial Hospital in Georgetown, South Carolina. Rose and her husband, Julius, lived just 15 miles from Georgetown, in a town called Andrews. For the previous decade, the civil rights movement had been gathering force. Just two years before Chris's birth, more than 200,000 people gathered to join the March on Washington in Washington, D.C., where they had the honor of listening to the Reverend Dr. Martin Luther King, Jr., deliver his "I Have a Dream" speech.

Race relations, though, remained tense in the United States, particularly in the South. Just ten years earlier in Montgomery, Alabama, Rosa Parks, a black woman, was arrested for refusing to give up her seat on a city bus to a white passenger. Two years later, in Little Rock, Arkansas, nine black students attempted to attend Central High School after the school had become

In Little Rock, Arkansas, an African-American boy watched a group of people, some carrying American flags, march to protest the admission of nine black students to Central High School in 1957. Chris Rock was born in South Carolina, and his parents experienced the oppressive atmosphere of segregation. They hoped for a life where they could achieve the American Dream. Their hopes took the family north—to Brooklyn, New York.

integrated. But when they tried to enter the school, the black students (who became known as the "Little Rock Nine)" were blocked from doing so on orders from the governor of Arkansas. Eventually, President Dwight D. Eisenhower deployed federal troops to protect the students as they entered the school.

Chris's mother, Rose, remembered what it was like to grow up in South Carolina as a child. She and her friends had to sit in a separate area at the soda shop and use a separate entrance (for "blacks only") to stores and restaurants. When Rose was a young woman, she worked as a cleaning lady for a white woman who constantly made sure that Rose was aware of her "place" in the house.

As the family grew, with the birth of two more boys, Andre and Tony, Rose and Julius Rock were interested in a new way of life for their children. The Rocks longed for a life where they could be treated equally and live the American Dream—that with hard work, courage, and determination, they could achieve prosperity. Given the oppressive atmosphere in South Carolina, the Rocks came to a life-changing conclusion—it was time to move north. When Chris was six years old, Julius and Rose packed up their three children and moved from Andrews, South Carolina, to Brooklyn, New York. Julius Rock was a hard-working, loving man. He drove a delivery truck for the *New York Daily News*. Rose, known for her big heart, taught special education for 17 years in the public schools in Brooklyn. At first, the family lived in an apartment in a section of the city called Crown Heights.

While living in Crown Heights, young Chris first became aware of his sense of humor. He gradually realized the effect his presentation of everyday occurrences had on people. He could make people laugh. Even when he wasn't trying, people found Chris's way of speaking and describing events funny. At the young age of six, Chris knew that comedy would forever be a part of his life. For a while, though, he wanted to be president of the United States, but his mother quickly put an end to that idea—she was worried that he would get shot if he ended up president. She wanted him to have a "regular" job, like a doctor or a teacher. So Chris dropped the idea of being the nation's highest political leader. And soon he thought about making comedy more than just part of his life—he thought about making it his whole life. By the time he was eight, Chris had decided he wanted to write comedy when he grew up.

LIFE IN BED-STUY

A few months after the move to Crown Heights, the family packed up again and moved to tree-lined Decatur Street, still in Brooklyn. The Rocks' brownstone house was in the

Bedford-Stuyvesant section, better known as "Bed-Stuy." Bed-Stuy was a tough neighborhood. The block that the Rocks lived on was not a bad one (Chris later described it as one of the nicest blocks in Bed-Stuy), but it was still three blocks from the projects and drug addicts and dealers. Chris saw firsthand the impact that drugs had on people's lives. Witnessing these horrors taught Chris an important life lesson: He learned to stay away from drugs. Rock later described crack cocaine as "… so addictive that if the new way to get high was to put it on a bullet, shoot it through a gun, and take a lick as it came out of the barrel, crackheads would try it." Chris opted not to try it.

Despite the nearby dangers outside his house, Chris grew up in a loving home with his five brothers and his sister: Andre, Tony, Brian, Kenny, Jordan, and Andrea. Chris and his brothers and sister all loved to laugh—as did their parents. Julius and Rose felt that it was important that their children find humor

Race Riot in Bedford-Stuyvesant

A year before Chris Rock was born, a riot broke out in his childhood neighborhood in New York City. On July 18, 1964, the Congress of Racial Equality (CORE) sponsored a protest in Harlem in Manhattan. The demonstrators were protesting the fatal shooting of 15-year-old James Powell, who was black, by a white police officer. The demonstration began peacefully, but as the evening went on, some of the protesters became violent and a riot broke out. The rioting in Harlem continued for two nights and then spread to the Brooklyn neighborhood of Bedford-Stuyvesant. When the riot finally ended, one person was dead, more than 100 people were injured, and hundreds more were arrested.

Later in the decade, even more serious riots in Detroit and the Watts section of Los Angeles would take place—resulting in a higher number of deaths, more injuries, and more arrests. The riots in Harlem and Bedford-Stuyvesant foreshadowed the racial tensions that would follow for years, including what Chris Rock would face when he entered James Madison High School some 15 years later.

in almost everything. They knew that a sense of humor would help them get through the tough times. The whole family enjoyed making one another laugh. Tony Rock, like Chris, would go on to become a comedian as an adult.

Growing up, Chris had his heroes. He loved watching Bill Cosby on television. Sometimes Chris would stay up late at night to watch Cosby when he was the guest host on *The Tonight Show*, sitting in for Johnny Carson. Chris thought that Cosby was unusually funny and witty. He got a kick out of Cosby's plaid suit and unique delivery of jokes. Chris also enjoyed television sitcoms. His favorites were *The Jeffersons*, *The Odd Couple*, *Newhart*, and *The Cosby Show*.

The shows Chris did not like were predictable sitcoms, like *The Love Boat* and *Three's Company*. Even at a young age, Chris was able to see through the weak plots and know what was going to happen ahead of time. This insight sometimes irritated his siblings when they were watching television with him, because Chris often spoiled the endings for them.

ROSE AND JULIUS ROCK

Chris Rock's family included two generations of preachers— his paternal grandfather and his paternal great-grandfather. Chris sometimes attended church with his grandfather, Allen. Allen Rock was a performer at heart with a big personality. Allen had a wild spirit and did not lead the stereotypical lifestyle of a preacher. He was loud and funny and sometimes dangerous and unpredictable. In an interview Chris Rock gave later in his life, he described how his grandfather had killed two people. The first man was a white bill collector. The man had walked uninvited into Allen's house in South Carolina and pushed aside the children to wake Allen and his wife. Allen shot him. (It was not uncommon at this time in this part of the United States for a white person to enter a black person's home uninvited.) After moving to New York, Allen shot the second man, who was trespassing through his yard.

Although Allen Rock was a wild card, Chris's parents were a steady presence in his life. Not all of the families in Chris's neighborhood had two parents; in fact, most were single-parent families. The influence of having two parents throughout his childhood would be a positive one for Chris. In interviews as an adult, Chris Rock spoke about the importance of just having his parents around while he was growing up. "If you were into rough stuff, it was rougher," he said in an interview about life in Bedford-Stuyvesant. "But if you're like me and had the two parents and rules and regulations in your house, it wasn't as tough."

The Rocks placed great value in spending time together—it did not even have to be so-called quality time—just time. The Rocks also taught their children to work hard and live by their moral values. They wanted their children to realize that they would have to do things better and work harder than white people if they hoped to succeed in life.

Rock's mother taught him the importance of caring for other people. She believed that people should be treated equally. As a young child, Rose knew she wanted to be a teacher—and she strove to ensure that all children had a chance to have the same education.

Rose and Julius Rock cared for 17 foster children throughout the years. Many families in Bedford-Stuyvesant took in foster children as an additional source of income. The Rocks did find the extra income useful, but much of the incentive behind taking in the foster children was Rose's great love of children and her desire to be surrounded by them. Some families treated their foster children poorly—making them sleep in the basement or eat a smaller amount of poorer-quality food than the families' own children. But Rose treated her foster children as her own. She believed that children who are frequently overlooked and neglected need the most help. As a schoolgirl, Rose used to bring soap in her bag and help the little children who hadn't bathed in days get clean, so they wouldn't be teased by their classmates.

Rose also taught her children that "association brings assimilation." In other words, it is important to choose your friends carefully, because you will act like those with whom you spend time. She urged her children to seek out friends with similar values and morals to their own. Rock later described his mother as a "ghetto snob." "She didn't teach us to believe we were as good as anybody else; she raised us to believe we were *better*," he said.

Julius was a diligent, hard-working man. Sometimes he had more than one job. Because he worked such long hours, he was often tired in the evenings. Later, Chris vowed to have the time and energy to play with own children—he did not want to be too tired to toss a ball around or play a game of tag.

Chris loved and respected his father a great deal. Julius believed in spanking his children when necessary—and Chris backs up this philosophy. Chris (as did his father) feels there are four times in a child's life when he or she needs a spanking: if the child steals, lies, cheats, or behaves disrespectfully toward another person.

Julius was careful with his money. The family had very little of it, so they had to watch how it was spent. Julius was quick to point out to his children how much it was costing him if they happened to spill a beverage or break something around the

IN HIS OWN WORDS...

Chris Rock and his family did not have much money while he was growing up. To make ends meet, Rock's parents were careful about how they spent their money. In his book, *Rock This!*, he wrote:

> We spent most of our shopping time in the no-frills aisle. You ever see the no-frills food? The white boxes, the black letters: RICE. No uncle, no riverboat, just rice. You look at the back of the box for the list of ingredients and it says look at the front of the box.

house. As an adult, Chris Rock would follow his father's example and become conservative with his finances. He described his outlook on money: "I inherited my parents' cheapness. I don't like owing anybody anything. I pay off the credit cards every month. I bought my car with cash."

Julius believed in giving your all, and he wanted his sons and daughter to grow up to be strong individuals in mind and spirit. That strength would be tested as Chris set out to begin school.

BROOKLYN EDUCATION

Segregation and racial tensions were still facts of life in the early 1970s in New York. Most people lived in black neighborhoods or white neighborhoods. As a result, schools became predominantly black or white. To try to end the segregation, the city required some students to be bused from their neighborhoods to attend schools in neighborhoods of another ethnic group. Chris Rock was one of these students. From the second grade on, he began boarding a bus that took him nearly an hour away from the all-black neighborhood of Bed-Stuy to an all-white neighborhood called Bensonhurst, on the other side of Brooklyn. Julius and Rose Rock, who placed great emphasis on education, believed that Chris would get a better education in a white school than he could get in a black school.

Bensonhurst, like Bed-Stuy, was a tough place to live. Crime and drugs were commonplace. Chris attended elementary school in Garrison Beach and then went to James Madison High School. Chris was one of the first black students to attend these schools. He was not met with warm smiles and open arms. Walking from the bus to the school, Chris passed picketers with signs containing racial epithets. Almost every day—from second grade through tenth grade—Chris was called names, teased, spit on, kicked, and sometimes beaten.

Some of the names that the students called Chris stemmed from his last name. Other names stemmed from his race.

For many years of his childhood, Chris spent nearly every school day witnessing some of the very worst in people. In one interview, years later, Rock described his school experience as being "like Vietnam." Race riots occurred at Chris's school through 1982.

Chris was not athletic, he was not popular, and he was not near the top of his class in academics. He did not like violence and did not try to fight back when he was beaten up; instead, Chris defended himself the best he knew how. He spent his school days trying to avoid ridicule from students and trying to stay awake. (Chris traveled nearly an hour each day on the school bus, so he had to wake up at 6:00 A.M., unlike his peers, who did not have to get up until 8:00 A.M.) Although Chris used his sense of humor with his family and friends at home, he dared not share it with the students of James Madison. There, Chris was shy and quiet. He spent most of his time avoiding the other students in hopes of not getting beaten or bullied.

Not only did Chris struggle in his all-white school, but he also did not get to know many youngsters from his own neighborhood because he was away from Bed-Stuy all day. So, outside of his family, Chris had few friends to confide in about the pressures and challenges he faced in school. The stress was intense. Chris wet his bed as a young boy and often spent his energy at school trying to shut out his surroundings.

IN HIS OWN WORDS...

Chris Rock did not like his name when he was growing up. His classmates used to tease him about it. Later, he told one interviewer:

It's my real name. My mother's name is Rose Rock. It was the worst name as a kid to have. They called me "Piece of the Rock," "Plymouth Rock," "Joe Rockid," and "Flintstones." ...Now they call me MISTER Rock.

Chris did find comfort from his siblings, parents, television, and music. He listened to a lot of rap and hip-hop. Sometimes he would sit out on his stoop and rap to entertain his brothers and sister and a few of the neighborhood children. The raps delighted the kids and gave Chris his first experiences of performing for an audience.

Occasionally, Chris's humor got him into trouble. Once, he got sent home from Bible school for laughing. Chris's mother, who had a good sense of humor herself, was not bothered by it. She knew Chris was a good person at heart. He was thoughtful and respectful to people around him. He had a responsible, caring side to him that Rose saw daily. As soon as Chris was able, he took on odd jobs—cleaning yards, shoveling snow, and delivering newspapers. He shared the money he made with his younger siblings.

By the time Chris had finished the tenth grade, he had had enough of James Madison High School. He had been coasting through school and did not see the point in continuing to put up with the unhappiness school brought. With the support of his parents, Rock dropped out of school at the age of 17.

Although Rock had had enough of the verbal—and sometimes physical—abuse he received from his peers, he did not give up on his education. Soon after dropping out, Rock studied for and earned his general equivalency diploma (G.E.D.). Later, Rock described getting his G.E.D.:

> You know what G.E.D. stands for? Good-Enough Diploma.... I don't get it. You mean I can make up four years in six hours? When you get a G.E.D., someone always has the nerve to say, 'Now you can go to college.' Hey, you can't go to a real college with a G.E.D. The only place that will take you is a community college. You know why they call it community college? Because it's like a disco with books. Anybody in the community can go: Crackheads, prostitutes, drug dealers. 'Come on in!'

After receiving his G.E.D., Rock did attend community college, where he studied broadcast journalism for one year. Perhaps he would one day be a newscaster. Between classes, Rock worked numerous jobs. Besides a stint at McDonald's, he was a busboy at Red Lobster (they had told him he wasn't good enough to become a waiter), an orderly at a mental hospital, a stock boy, and a laborer for the *New York Daily News*, the company for which his father worked.

Rock was dissatisfied with the work, so he passed the time by telling jokes to his coworkers. Rock loved to make people laugh and found that people were often laughing when they were around him. It made him feel good. Rock did not stay long at any one job. What he was really hoping for was a job in New York City's comedy club scene.

FINDING HIS WAY IN COMEDY

One of Rock's pastimes as a teenager was to follow the careers of two of his idols: boxer Sugar Ray Leonard and comedian Eddie Murphy. In 1985, when Rock was 20, he stood in line to buy a ticket for Murphy's stand-up comedy show at Radio City Music Hall. While Rock waited to get to the counter, he read in a newspaper that Catch a Rising Star, a famous comedy club, was planning an open-mike session. Rock thought this might be his chance. He was right.

Catch a Rising Star first opened its doors in 1972. Robin Williams, Rosie O'Donnell, Jerry Seinfeld, and Ray Romano were a few of the people who launched their careers at Catch a Rising Star. When Chris Rock auditioned during open-mike night at this popular club, the audience loved him. He became a regular performer there and also began making the rounds at other comedy clubs in New York City.

When he wasn't able to get a spot at a comedy club, Rock just hung around. He enjoyed the atmosphere at the clubs and knew that it sometimes paid off just to be in the right place at the right time.

Eddie Murphy is shown performing his stand-up act in March 1985 at Radio City Music Hall in Manhattan. Murphy was one of Chris Rock's idols. While he was waiting in line to buy tickets for Murphy's show, Rock read about open-mike auditions at Catch a Rising Star, a New York comedy club. He decided to give the tryouts a shot.

At one club in Manhattan, the Comic Strip, Rock would find odd jobs to do, like stacking chairs at the end of the night, just to be in the building. This comedy club had been a launching pad for Eddie Murphy, as well other comic greats, like Seinfeld and George Carlin. The Comic Strip's mission is to find the best young comedians in New York, help them develop their talent, and prepare them to go on to television or film. Rock knew the importance of playing at the Comic Strip—a good performance there could propel his career into the big leagues. In his early days at the Comic Strip, Rock did not always get a prime-time slot at the microphone, but he stuck around until he had his chance. Even being on at 2:00 A.M. was better than not being on at all. The appearances gave Rock practice and allowed him to work on his routine and perfect his talent.

Within a year, Rock was performing regularly at a number of New York comedy clubs. During his gigs, Rock honed his delivery and improved his stage presence. His expanding comedic skills paid off. The people loved him. One night at the Comic Strip, a particular member of the audience was impressed with Rock's performance. That person was none other than Rock's idol, Eddie Murphy.

Murphy recognized Rock's budding talent and offered him a spot on *Uptown Comedy Express,* an HBO special that featured Rock and four other up-and-coming comedians: Arsenio Hall, Barry Sobel, Robert Townsend, and Marsha Warfield. Murphy also got Rock a small role in *Beverly Hills Cop II,* directed by Tony Scott. In the film, Rock played a valet at the Playboy Mansion. Although the roles were small, Rock could now add television and film credits to his résumé.

Sam Kinison, another comedian, also noticed Rock during one of his stand-up routines in those early years in New York City. One evening at Catch a Rising Star, Rock was making a joke that no one in the audience was laughing at, except for one person sitting in the back of the club. After the show, Rock was introduced to that person: It was Kinison, who said he thought Rock was very funny. Kinison was making a guest appearance on *Saturday Night Live* and invited Rock to join him. Rock had a great experience seeing the show live for the first time. Malcolm-Jamal Warner was the host that night.

Rock felt that Kinison's invitation to attend *Saturday Night Live* was one of the nicest gestures anyone had made toward him. He and Kinison became friends. Like Rock, Kinison came from a long line of preachers. And rather than follow in his relatives' footsteps, Kinison followed his own dream— comedy. In the 1980s, Kinison was known as one of the rudest and loudest comedians performing. He shocked audiences with his views on religion and women. He appeared in HBO

One of Chris Rock's earliest mentors was Sam Kinison, one of the most raucous comedians performing in the late 1980s. Rock admired Kinison's style and would later incorporate some of Kinison's preacher-like theatrics into his own act.

cable specials, and on *Saturday Night Live* and *In Living Color*, another sketch comedy show. Kinison was also a heavy drug and alcohol abuser. Joking about his addiction became part of his act.

Although Kinison became Rock's professional mentor, Rock was not a drug user and he had no interest in being one. Knowing all too well the tragic consequences, Rock felt that drugs were just plain dumb. Kinison's actions reinforced those beliefs. Just like back in Bed-Stuy, Rock watched the effects of drugs on a human life and knew he wanted to stay clean.

Looking beyond the addiction, Rock appreciated Kinison's stage style and would incorporate some of Kinison's preacher-like repetition, volume, and theatrics into his own routine. Rock thought of Kinison as a white Richard Pryor. Kinison was honest and willing to try new ideas—even if taking a chance meant not always being popular with the mainstream.

In 1988, Chris Rock landed a role in another film, called *I'm Gonna Git You Sucka*, directed by Keenan Ivory Wayans. Rock played a rib-joint customer. The part was small, but Rock was noticed and remembered by fans. Arsenio Hall enjoyed Rock's performance so much that Hall offered him a spot on *The Arsenio Hall Show*.

Then Rock suffered a hard blow in 1989. His father died from complications following a ruptured ulcer. Rock had deep respect for his father and missed him greatly. Julius had supported Rock's decisions throughout his life and had been a constant presence. Now he was gone. Rock contemplated giving up his comedy dream and taking on a steadier career. He wanted to contribute to his family and help earn enough money for them; stand-up comedy was not bringing in enough to do that. But after considerable thought, Rock decided to continue to follow his dream.

3

Saturday Night Live

After appearing on _The Arsenio Hall Show_, Chris Rock caught the attention of Lorne Michaels, the executive producer of NBC's _Saturday Night Live_. Rock tried out during a mass audition, got the part, and joined the cast in 1990. He now had a regular spot on a popular television show.

For the next three years, Rock would be coming to his fans live. _Saturday Night Live_ is a late-night comedy show, consisting of short skits, fake news segments, commercial parodies, and a musical guest. _SNL_ first aired on October 11, 1975, with George Carlin as the host. Over the years, its cast of regular performers changed several times. When Rock joined the cast, so did newcomers Tim Meadows, Adam Sandler, Chris Farley, David Spade, and Julia Sweeney.

ON THE SET

Rock's best memories of his time at _SNL_ are those involving his friends—Farley, Sandler, Spade, and Meadows. Rock shared a dressing room with Farley, who would become a close friend over the next few years. Rock thought Farley was one of the funniest people he had ever known. Rock's mother, Rose, became friends with Farley's mother after the two met at a Mother's Day Special for *Saturday Night Live*. The two mothers continued to stay in touch long after their sons left the show.

Although Rock had a good gig at *SNL*, he faced some discrimination on the set. If he walked around in sweats and a T-shirt or jeans and an old shirt, the security guards were sure to ask to see some ID. So Rock got into the habit of dressing sharply at all times—he often came to the set of *Saturday Night Live* in a crisp shirt and jacket.

In 1991, fans of the show enjoyed Rock's portrayal of Luther Campbell, of the music group 2 Live Crew, in "The Sinatra Group" sketch, which also featured the following characters: Frank Sinatra (played by Phil Hartman), Sinéad O'Connor (played by Jan Hooks), Billy Idol (played by Sting), Steve Lawrence (played by Mike Myers), and Eydie Gorme (played by Victoria Jackson). In 1992, Rock had people laughing with "Chris Rock's White Person's Guide to Surviving the Apollo" and "The Bensonhurst Dating Game." Some of Rock's funniest characters included Nat X of "The Dark Side With Nat X" and Onski from "I'm Chillin'."

A few years after leaving *Saturday Night Live*, Rock returned to the show as a guest host. During this episode in 1996, he played Nat X. Rock began his Nat X segment by saying, "Peace, brothers and sisters. I'm Nat X, and welcome to 'The Dark Side,' the only 15-minute show on TV. Why only 15 minutes? 'Cause if the man gave me any more, he would consider that welfare." Nat X sketches would later be included in the video *Saturday Night Live: The Best of Chris Rock*.

Rock, Farley, Sandler, Spade, and Rob Schneider became known as the "Bad Boys" of *Saturday Night Live*. These five rising stars often did sketches together and became known for their wild, outrageous, and fast-paced comedy. All five would go on to do more television and film after *Saturday Night Live*.

Despite Rock's successes on *SNL*, he also faced some criticism. Reviewers wrote that Rock was not putting enough effort into his roles. Years later, Rock agreed with this assessment in interviews. He described his time at *Saturday Night Live* as the "awkward years." Rock was relishing the nightlife. He was dating many women and enjoying the perks that came with being on television and in the movies. He had had it hard during his school years; now that he was on his own and building a career, he wanted to let loose and live a little. Unfortunately, his nightlife activities made it hard for him to focus clearly when he showed up to work. If he did not feel like working, he skipped rehearsals altogether. This mind-set was not helping his performance on *Saturday Night Live*.

Rock later blamed himself for the criticism he received at *SNL*; he said in one interview: "I was just happy to be there.... I go into things really prepared now, where in the old days I was definitely winging it." At this point in time, Rock was not taking his job—or his life—seriously.

DEVELOPING A FOLLOWING

Despite Rock's happy-go-lucky attitude in these early years of his career, he was slowly, but steadily, building a fan base. He did try to take care when he chose his roles and gigs. Rock was beginning to make a name for himself—he was not following in another comedian's footsteps or blindly accepting any opportunity that came his way. He appeared in many television and video recordings just before and during his time on *Saturday Night Live*. Some of these appearances included *Comedy's Dirtiest Dozen*, a comedy concert film, and *Who Is Chris Rock?*, which he taped with his mother. A few of his television guest appearances included *Miami Vice* and *The Fresh Prince of Bel-Air*.

Besides *Saturday Night Live* and his other television appearances, Rock continued to take occasional film roles. In 1991,

Chris Rock and Chris Farley fielded questions in September 1990 at a press conference held to announce that they were joining the cast of *Saturday Night Live*. Rock thought that Farley was one of the funniest people he had met. The two comedians, who shared a dressing room, became good friends. Even their mothers became close.

Chris Rock showed a more dramatic side in the 1991 independent film *New Jack City*. In the movie, directed by Mario Van Peebles, Rock played Pookie, a young crack addict who was asked by the police to go undercover to help apprehend a drug lord. To prepare for the role, Rock spent time with a drug addict.

he appeared in Mario Van Peebles's *New Jack City* with Wesley Snipes. The movie became the highest-grossing independent feature film that year. Rock played a young crack addict named Pookie, who goes through rehabilitation and is then asked to go undercover for two police officers who hope to bring down a cocaine lord. To prepare, he spent several days with a Brooklyn drug addict to learn his habits and traits. His performance in the film attracted much attention. Critics appreciated his ability to deliver serious lines with a comic twist. Film critic Roger Ebert called Rock's performance "effortlessly authentic and convincing."

Rock also released *Born Suspect,* his first comedy album, in 1991. He recorded the album in Atlanta. His comedy about the minimum wage, politicians and crack, and women laid the groundwork for what was to come in his later routines. Although his delivery would improve over the years, the wit and honesty of his humor was evident in his early work.

Then in 1992, Rock had a small role in an Eddie Murphy film called *Boomerang*, in which he played a character named Bony T. Rock later told Larry King in an interview that he felt as if his and Murphy's roles in *Boomerang*—Rock works in the mailroom of a company owned by Murphy—were much like their relationship in real life.

Later in the year, Rock received some sad news: Sam Kinison was dead. Although his friend and mentor had for years continued his abuse of drugs and alcohol, he had finally realized his addictions would one day kill him. Kinison decided to turn his life around by getting sober and staying clean. Unfortunately, not long after he had begun this new life, a vehicle driven by a drunken teenager hit his car. The crash killed Kinison and injured his wife, Malika Souiri.

Back at *Saturday Night Live*, Rock was not happy. He was feeling a lot of pressure to live up to the greats who came before him: Eddie Murphy, John Belushi, and Dan Aykroyd. In addition, Rock was used to performing his own material—until now, he had written all of his comedy for his stand-up gigs. At *SNL*, Rock had to depend on the writing staff, which happened to be nearly all white. The writers at the show did

DID YOU KNOW?

Chris Rock thinks carefully about which projects he takes on and which ones he turns down. In 1993, Paramount Pictures offered him a part in a film called *Sanford and Son*. The movie would have been based on the 1970s television sitcom of the same name. Paramount hoped that Rock would take the role of Lamont Sanford, the son. Rock called the idea "insane," and he lobbied to have the film stopped. The production was halted.

The cast of *Saturday Night Live* posed on the set at the start of the 1992–1993 season. They were (from left, front row) Chris Farley, Al Franken, and Melanie Hutsell; (from left, middle row) Chris Rock, Julia Sweeney, Dana Carvey, and Rob Schneider; (from left, back row) Adam Sandler, David Spade, Ellen Cleghorne, Kevin Nealon, Phil Hartman, and Tim Meadows. Increasingly, Rock felt that the show was not making the most of his abilities.

not always see eye to eye with Rock, and Rock was left unable to produce the comedy he wanted.

During the period that Rock was on *Saturday Night Live*, the cast also included Dana Carvey, Mike Myers, Dennis Miller, and Phil Hartman. All had developed popular characters that audiences wanted to see, show after show. "When I got there, there were stars, real stars," Rock said in the book *Live From New York: An Uncensored History of Saturday Night Live, As Told By Its Stars, Writers and Guests.* "There were a lot of big people on the show. So for me to not get on wasn't that big a deal."

Rock's air time seemed to be limited in other ways, too. "With Tim Meadows being on the show, you know somewhere in your mind that if there's two nonwhite, pretty good sketches, they probably won't both get on," Rock said in *Live From New York*. "And they'll never go back to back, even if they have nothing to do with each other."

By 1993, Rock felt that his abilities were not being used on the show. In one interview, Rock later stated that he "felt like the adopted [black] kid with great white parents." Rock decided it was time for a change. He left *Saturday Night Live*.

He left it, though, with lasting friendships and an impact on his career. Rock said in *Live From New York*:

> Was being on the show the greatest creative experience for me? No. But it's still the biggest thing that ever happened to me in show business. The jump from broke to famous is the biggest jump. *Saturday Night Live* brands you as a professional. No matter what is written about me to this day, *SNL* comes up. It's the Harvard of Comedy.

When Rock started looking at other opportunities, he found one in a chief competitor of *SNL*, Keenan Ivory Wayans's *In Living Color*, which first aired in 1990. The Fox network show, with a primarily black cast, was a good fit for Rock. He was not an official cast member, but he appeared in nine episodes as a guest star, and he always felt at home on the set. During his time on the show, he was able to bring back his character, "Cheap Pete," from the movie *I'm Gonna Git You Sucka*. Unfortunately, *In Living Color* got canceled in 1994, soon after Rock started making guest appearances during the show's fifth season.

4

After Saturday Night Live

By the time he left *Saturday Night Live*, Chris Rock had already undertaken stand-up comedy, television, and film. In 1993, he tried new endeavors: writing screenplays and coproducing. He created, wrote, produced, and starred in a movie called *CB4*, a satire made by Universal Pictures. The rap comedy, directed by Tamra Davis, opened No. 1 at the box office, and was well-received by critics. The film follows the rise to fame of a rap group called CB4.

Rock added a few bits to the movie for his fans. In one scene, Rock re-enacts his crack-smoking scene from *New Jack City*, complete with the same facial expressions. In a narration during the film, Rock compares the character of Gusto to Nino Brown, who was the main drug lord in *New Jack City*. At the end of the movie, Rock's character quibbles with Isaac Hayes's character. These two actors had had a similar dialogue in *I'm Gonna Git You Sucka*, where Rock played a customer in Hayes's rib joint.

Chris Rock appears with Khandi Alexander in a scene from CB4. The movie is a mock documentary that follows a rap group called CB4 as it achieves stardom. Rock also wrote the screenplay and was a coproducer of the film. The movie opened number one at the box office.

IN LOVE

In 1993, Rock and a couple of his friends attended the Essence Awards, an annual event that was first held seven years earlier to honor the achievements of black women.

At the awards show, Rock met a young woman named Malaak Compton, a Howard University graduate. She had worked for a short time in the cosmetics industry and then accepted a position as public relations coordinator for the U.S. Committee for UNICEF. Rock and Compton began dating and soon fell in love.

With a steady, loving relationship, Rock was feeling good about his personal life and his career. In 1993, Rock was offered his first HBO special, *Chris Rock: Big Ass Jokes*. The 30-minute stand-up routine, performed in Atlanta, won a CableACE Award in the category of "best stand-up comedy

Comedy Influences

Chris Rock has had a number of comedic idols over the years. A few of them gained acclaim around the same time—the 1960s. Yet they had their own distinctive styles and followed different paths to fame. Another of his idols is more of a contemporary and helped Rock get his start. The following are a few of the stars who influenced Rock:

• Richard Pryor, who died in December 2005 at the age of 65, was a comic storyteller known for his use of profanity and his fearless look at race and modern customs. Early in his career, he was a much milder comic, and he did not develop his more caustic material until the late 1960s and 1970s. Pryor starred in a number of popular movies, including *Silver Streak*, *Which Way Is Up?*, *The Toy*, and *Stir Crazy*. In 1980, he set himself on fire while freebasing cocaine. He later incorporated the accident in his stand-up. He announced he had multiple sclerosis in 1986 and gave his last live performance in 1992. In 1998, he won the first Mark Twain Prize for American Humor, presented by the Kennedy Center.

• George Carlin earned acclaim for his irreverent attitude and his views on language, religion, and many taboo subjects. He got his start on television variety shows. By the late 1960s, though, he changed his appearance, with longer hair and a beard, as well as his routines. His most famous routine, "Seven Words You Can Never Say on Television," appeared on his 1972 comedy album *Class Clown*. Carlin's first HBO special was shown in 1977, and he continued doing HBO specials every year or two into the early 1990s. A new generation discovered him around that time with special." Rock had been up against D.L. Hughley and Margaret Cho, two rising comedy stars. Winning the award meant a lot to Rock; he had never won anything before. Critics and fans alike loved the show. Critics pointed out how wasted Rock's talent had been on *Saturday Night Live*. The HBO special highlighted what Rock could deliver: edgy, honest comedy. Though the special was successful, his performance lacked the punchy delivery and showmanship needed to set Rock apart from other comedians.

In 1995, Rock appeared as Deke Anthony in the film *The Immortals* and as Yuck Mouth in the film *Panther*.

his appearance in the film *Bill and Ted's Excellent Adventure*. He was named No. 2 on Comedy Central's list of the 100 greatest stand-ups, just behind Pryor.

• Bill Cosby began his stand-up career in the 1960s. Unlike other comedians, Cosby told more stories than jokes, stories about growing up in Philadelphia. And he avoided profanity, too. He was the first African-American actor to star in a drama series, *I Spy* (1965–1968). His animated series, *Fat Albert and the Cosby Kids*, was based on his childhood, too, and was popular in the 1970s. The next decade saw *The Cosby Show*, which ran on NBC from 1984 to 1992. The sitcom was No. 1 in the ratings for five straight seasons. Another series, *Cosby*, ran on CBS from 1996 to 2000. Cosby has had six platinum comedy albums, and he has written several best-selling books, including *Fatherhood* and *Time Flies*.

• At 19, Eddie Murphy joined the cast of *Saturday Night Live* in 1980, and he became a breakout star the following season. He created some of the show's best-known characters of the time, like the former child movie star Buckwheat and a life-size version of Gumby. His movie career began to take off with roles in *48 Hrs.* and *Trading Places*. Murphy stayed on *SNL* until 1984. That year, he was in the huge hit film *Beverly Hills Cop*, which cemented his stardom. From 1989 to the mid-1990s, his film career hit a slump, but it turned around with *The Nutty Professor* in 1996. Since then, his family-friendly films (like the *Shrek* movies) have done better at the box office than his films geared toward adult audiences.

The Immortals was directed by Brian Grant. In this heist-gone-wrong action film, Rock starred with Tony Curtis, Eric Roberts, Tia Carrere, and Joe Pantoliano. *Panther*, directed by Mario Van Peebles, highlighted the lives of the 1960s activist group called the Black Panthers. The film was relatively well-reviewed, but Rock did not have a major role in it. Still, Rock persevered. He knew that, by following in his father's footsteps and continuing to work hard, he could, eventually reach stardom.

TREADING WATER

Overall, Rock's career had slowed. In the previous two years, he had produced little. His goal was to make it big. He wanted to get on a television series, but he was not getting any offers. Rock continued to take movie roles, but they were not of great quality; he took them to pay his bills—not to showcase his talent. In April 1995, Rock decided to leave his agent at the William Morris Agency. Unfortunately he had failed to get a new agent first—and now found himself with no representation. Every agent Rock visited turned down the chance to represent him.

The year 1996, though, marked a turning point for Rock. First, he made a commitment to improve his comedy. He studied, with a new vigor, the greats before him—Bill Cosby, Woody Allen, and Richard Pryor, to name a few. Rock also remembered his grandfather, Allen Rock, and the charisma and flair that emanated from his sermons. Rock realized that it wasn't enough to string a line of jokes together. The jokes themselves needed to be of consistently high quality. If he did one good joke and then two bad jokes, the first joke would lose its impact. So he needed to get rid of the bad jokes and keep only the compelling ones. He also needed to improve his delivery. To do this, he learned to repeat key phrases over and over, adding emphasis and laying the base for a joke's setup. This practice added dramatic flair and charisma—qualities that helped set him apart from other comics. His realization and dedicated follow-through greatly improved his comedy.

SUCCESS FROM "BRING THE PAIN"

Wanting to showcase his improved comedy and delivery, Rock made a comedy special for HBO called *Chris Rock: Bring the Pain*, which he taped in Washington, D.C., at the Takoma Theatre. The Takoma Theatre first opened in 1923 and had flourished for many years as a cinema theater. In the 1980s it was sold to a new owner, who turned it into a stage for live performances. By 1996, however, the theater was presenting very few performances. Rock's HBO special was Takoma's first big show in a long time.

Rock looked at this special as his last shot to get famous—he put his all into creating a show that people would talk about and remember. The title *Bring the Pain* came from a song by the rapper Method Man (Clifford Smith). In this special, Rock talked about the divided response among blacks to O.J. Simpson, women, domestic abuse, and Marion Barry (the mayor of Washington, D.C., who was a known crack user).

Rock's ideas about race, including one segment in which he talks about some differences among black people, became popular with both black and white people alike. Rock challenges one small group of black people: those, he says, who have given up their responsibilities. Rock says the worst thing about them is that they love to *not know*—to be ignorant. This group, in turn, ruins opportunities for all other black people, who are just trying to make a life for themselves.

In *Bring the Pain*, Rock also talks about race relations between whites and blacks, including the unlikelihood of a black person's ever becoming president. He jokes:

> Colin Powell can't win. Colin Powell has a better chance
> of winning the bronze in female gymnastics.... White
> people aren't voting for Colin Powell. Say they are—they

are not.... White people say they going to vote for him because it seems like the right thing to say.... Just like if you ask someone if they want to be an organ donor. They always say 'yeah.' Nobody wants to be an organ donor. Nobody. It just seems like the right thing to say.

Bring the Pain was a huge success. Big comedy concerts had nearly disappeared—*Bring the Pain* was a rebirth for the comedy concert. It was also a rebirth for Rock. People were suddenly comparing him to Eddie Murphy and Richard Pryor. The show won two Emmy Awards: outstanding writing for a variety or music program, and outstanding variety, music, or comedy special. Rock's mother was at the Emmy ceremony to watch her eldest son accept his awards. She was overcome with happiness and pride.

Bring the Pain was also made into a video. DreamWorks Records released a CD, *Roll With the New*, which featured material from *Bring the Pain* as well as musical bits and comedy sketches. *Roll With the New* won a Grammy for best spoken comedy album.

Rose Rock

Following the death of her husband, Julius, in 1989, Rose Rock moved back to South Carolina in March 1993. She lives a quiet life there in Myrtle Beach, in a home that Chris bought for her. Rose still surrounds herself with children; she runs a day-care center called First Steps Day Care in Maryville, South Carolina. She spends her spare time reading the works of authors like Maya Angelou and James Baldwin and writing. She keeps in touch with her seven children and is pleased about Chris's professional success and his happiness in marriage.

Rose enjoys keeping up with Chris's career and watching it blossom. As a result of his fame, she has had opportunities she might not have had, like meeting Oprah Winfrey. Along with many other celebrity mothers, Rose also provided a menu item at Caroline's Comedy Club in New York. According to Rose, the dish is Chris's favorite—"smothered chicken and gravy." When she prepares the dish, she simmers chicken with scallions, onions, and celery and serves it with hot biscuits and gravy.

Chris Rock and Malaak Compton-Rock attend the Grammy Awards in 1998 at Radio City Music Hall. The couple met in 1993 at the Essence Awards. Three years later, they were married in Oxon Hill, Maryland.

"Champagne," a song from the CD, became popular on MTV and radio stations. Rock was getting more and more opportunities to appear in movies and on television. He appeared on *The Tonight Show* and *The Rosie O'Donnell Show,* among others. *Bring the Pain* took Rock's career to a new level—Rock was becoming a star.

Rock covered the 1996 presidential elections for *Politically Incorrect*, then on Comedy Central. The show, hosted by Bill Maher, gathered four guests to talk about politically sensitive issues. During Rock's coverage as an Indecision '96 correspondent, he offered his own take on the presidential primaries, the Democratic National Convention, the Republican National Convention, and Election Night. His contribution to the show earned him an Emmy nomination in 1997 for outstanding writing for a variety or music program.

Rock took on two television commercials: 1-800-Collect and Nike. In the Nike ads, Rock gave voice to the puppet Li'l Penny, the alter ego of Orlando Magic basketball star Anfernee "Penny" Hardaway. Rock did more than 30 commercials as the mechanical live-action puppet. Unlike Rock, who lived a relatively simple lifestyle, Li'l Penny went all out: The puppet had a $50,000 wardrobe.

SETTLING DOWN

Three years had passed since Rock met Malaak Compton at the Essence Awards. The couple wanted to marry and did so on November 23, 1996, in Oxon Hill, Maryland. On the invitations, Rock dedicated the wedding ceremony to his father.

Like most newlyweds, the couple had their share of early struggles as they worked to make a life together. Rock's career really took off over the next year, and he had to work long hours to fulfill his commitments. The marriage suffered as a result. But the couple worked together and created a solid, loving relationship. Rock credits his wife with helping to center his life.

The Rocks bought a house in Brooklyn. With their little dog, Essence (named after the award show), the newlyweds were ready to begin a new stage of their lives. Paying a mortgage each month brought a new sense of responsibility to Rock. He responded by working twice as hard. He wanted to ensure financial stability and security for him and his wife.

5

The Chris Rock Show

After the success of *Bring the Pain*, *Politically Incorrect,* and his television commercials, Chris Rock was on a roll. He started making guest appearances on hit television shows—among them *Martin* and *Homicide: Life on the Street.* Once in a while, Rock took on a project that really flopped, like a movie he made with Steve Martin called *Sgt. Bilko.* Rock, though, was working hard and maintaining a very busy schedule.

When television networks approached him with the opportunity to write his own show, Rock jumped at the chance. At last he would have the chance to incorporate his stand-up routines into a comedy show for television. His childhood dream of becoming a comedy writer was taking shape.

The Chris Rock Show was a talk show written by and starring Rock. It became one of HBO's highest-rated programs and ran from 1997 to 2000. The show had an opening monologue, interviews, stand-up comedy, and live music.

The show allowed Rock to stay on top of current events and entertain and inform the public in the way he loved—through stand-up and sketch comedy. Rock wrote out ideas and scripts on yellow legal pads (he wasn't much of a computer guy at the time) and then tossed his ideas around with the other writers from the show. Rock took his job seriously. He researched, he rehearsed, and he delivered. Compared with the young, happy-go-lucky man he had been on *Saturday Night Live*, Rock was a new man—more mature and more professional. And that made him a better comedian.

Rock's show also gave him the opportunity to showcase his idols, like comedian George Carlin. While growing up, Rock greatly admired Carlin's work, and he was happy to book him for the show. Carlin is known for challenging conventional norms by pointing out the absurdities that surround many social norms. Rock's own social commentaries on controversial topics have led to comparisons between him and Carlin. Other guests on the show included Jesse Jackson, Puff Daddy, Whoopi Goldberg, Johnnie Cochran, Bernie Mac, fellow Bed-Stuy resident Spike Lee, and Lenny Kravitz, to name a few.

BUILDING A WRITING TEAM

Rock hired several people to help him come up with and write material for *The Chris Rock Show*. Ali LeRoi, Wanda Sykes, Mike Upchurch, John Marshall, and Lance Crouther were a few of these writers. Rock's brother Tony also did some writing for the 30-minute program. Rock had met many of the writers he hired during club gigs in years past. Some had opened for Rock.

One of the writers closest to Rock was Ali LeRoi. LeRoi, whose dreadlocks spill down his back, grew up in Chicago. Rock and LeRoi met in the early 1990s, when they were both making a name for themselves. They both liked cutting-edge comedy. At the time Rock approached LeRoi to write for his show, LeRoi was writing material for comedian Bernie Mac

Ali LeRoi was one of the writers hired for *The Chris Rock Show*. LeRoi could take Rock's ideas and craft great routines from them. "He knows how to find the gold in the dirt," Rock said of LeRoi. Their collaboration would continue for many years to come.

and opening for him. They became very good friends over the years. Like Rock, LeRoi had felt like an outcast as a child—he was not into the typical entertainment that black youths in his neighborhood enjoyed. LeRoi had grown up watching primarily white comedians like Dick Van Dyke, Carol Burnett, and George Carlin on television.

The duo of Rock and LeRoi made a strong writing team. Rock threw out bits and pieces of inspired ideas, and LeRoi would sort out those thoughts and turn them into a cohesive comedy routine or sketch. "He knows how to find the gold in the dirt," Rock said about LeRoi. Together, they were able to produce high-quality, fast-paced humor, which was exactly what *The Chris Rock Show* aimed to generate.

AN ALBUM AND A BOOK

Rock's comedy album *Roll With the New* appeared in stores in 1997. Most of the album is stand-up, but some skits and songs are included as well. This varied content came about, in part, because of Adam Sandler's influence on Rock. Sandler had gone on to make his own comedy albums—developing unique, original material and presenting a mix of songs, skits, and comedy. Rock heard Sandler's records and found them interesting. He wanted to try something similar—something no other black comic had tried.

Rock also wrote an autobiographical book, *Rock This!*, published by Hyperion in 1997. Much of the book contained material from his stand-up routines, but he also wrote about his childhood, growing up in Bed-Stuy, and his life after school. The dedication in the book read, "For my dad, Julius Rock. The funniest guy I've ever known." The book was a huge success and spent time on the *New York Times* and the *Wall Street Journal* bestseller lists.

The year continued with Rock playing a small role in a slapstick movie with Chris Farley. The movie, *Beverly Hills Ninja*, was directed by Dennis Dugan. Farley plays a character assumed to be the legendary "Great White Ninja." The movie received mostly negative reviews.

On September 4, 1997, Rock was the host of the MTV Music Video Awards at Radio City Music Hall in New York City. The award show had the third-highest ratings in its history. Rock was honored to be asked to host the show and had great fun at the awards. In his opening monologue, he joked, "The Spice Girls sold 10 million records? How come I don't know anyone who bought one?" Although parts of his monologue shocked some viewers and the network had to bleep out some profanity, MTV president Judy McGrath defended Rock's performance by saying that the MTV audience liked a little danger and risk. The show was hoping to pull in young viewers, and Rock helped accomplish that.

The year ended sadly for Rock. Chris Farley, his good friend, colleague, and former *Saturday Night Live* star, died of an accidental cocaine and heroin overdose in his Chicago apartment. He was 33. On December 23, Rock, along with hundreds of others, attended Farley's wake and funeral in Madison, Wisconsin. Rock would miss Farley's original humor and friendship. "He was one of my best friends and one of the funniest guys I've ever known," Rock said soon after Farley's death. "I love him, and I'm going to miss him."

IN HIS OWN WORDS...

Chris Rock has seen people from his old neighborhood and friends in show business lose their lives to drugs. He wants no part of drugs or their destructive effects. He may joke about drugs in his stand-up act, but he also tries to shed light on the absurdities of taking drugs:

> I don't get high, but sometimes I wish I did. That way, when I messed up in life I would have an excuse. But right now there's no rehab for stupidity.
> —from *Rock This!*

> Actually, I think all addiction starts with soda. Every junkie did soda first. But no one counts that. Maybe they should. The soda connection is clear. Why isn't a presidential commission looking into this? Or at least some guys from the National Carbonation Council.
> —from *Rock This!*

> Do you know what the good side of crack is? If you're up at the right hour, you can get a VCR for $1.50. You can furnish your whole house for $10.95.
> —from *Bring the Pain*

RECOGNITION

In 1998, *The Chris Rock Show* was nominated for an Emmy in writing. Rock continued to put a great deal of time and effort into the show—always looking to maintain the quality of its content. He worked from an office in Midtown Manhattan. In his office, he displayed Woody Allen posters on the walls, art books on the tables, and his favorite music in the CD racks. All of these things—performers, art, and music—inspired Rock to create his comedy. When Rock looked over ideas from other writers on the show, he was thinking about what was going to make him laugh. He wanted to see topics that weren't funny that he could *make* funny. He found a challenge in taking a serious or depressing issue and making people laugh about it.

Besides staying busy with the hit television show, Rock also made more movies. During the summer of 1998, Rock played roles in *Lethal Weapon 4* (opposite Mel Gibson and Danny Glover) and *Dr. Dolittle* (opposite Eddie Murphy). Each movie grossed more than 100 million dollars.

In *Lethal Weapon 4*, Rock played Detective Lee Butters. For this role, Rock was nominated for an American Comedy Award as funniest supporting actor in a motion picture. Critics applauded the energy and excitement that Rock lent to the film.

In *Dr. Dolittle*, the remake of the 1967 movie, Rock was the voice of the outspoken guinea pig, Rodney. Film critic Roger Ebert noted that Rock's character got most of the laughs in the movie, and other critics wrote that Rodney was the cutest of the animals.

In May 1999, the satire film *Dogma* debuted at the Cannes Film Festival in France. In it, Rock played the thirteenth apostle, Rufus, who—according to the film—had been left out of the Bible because he was black. Making *Dogma* was hard work. The cast, which included Matt Damon, Ben Affleck, Salma Hayek, and fellow comedian George Carlin, spent two weeks in rehearsals, six intense hours a day, before filming began. Rock was excited to work with the film's director, Kevin Smith. The two got along very well. The movie received mixed reviews, but Rock still had a successful year.

BIGGER AND BLACKER

Besides acting, Rock also enjoyed behind-the-scenes entertainment jobs. He was the executive producer of a family sitcom called *The Hughleys*, which ran from 1998 to 2000 on ABC and from 2000 to 2002 on UPN. The star of the show, D.L. Hughley, had grown up in Los Angeles. He was expelled from high school and joined a gang called the Bloods. When his cousin was shot (as a result of gang activity), Hughley decided to turn his life around and ended up doing stand-up comedy.

Also in 1999, Rock did another HBO comedy special, called *Bigger & Blacker*. His previous special, *Bring the Pain*, had been a huge success. Rock had to ask himself: How do you follow that? Put on a bigger show? Perform at a prestigious theater, like Radio City Music Hall? No. Not Chris Rock. He filmed his special at the Apollo Theater in Harlem, New York. "Black is always associated with small," Rock said in an interview. "Nothing's ever been bigger and blacker—*ever*. That's what I wanted to say: You can be that." And Rock delivered. He joked about everything from relationships to impeachment to neglected children. His words cut to the chase; he was brutally honest and witty.

One reason Rock enjoys doing these kinds of HBO shows (which are filmed in front of a live audience in a theater, shown on HBO as a comedy special, and then released as comedy albums and on DVDs) is that he has more freedom to say what he wants and is able to take more chances. Because of this, Rock invests a lot of time and concentration into each special he produces. He wants his comedy to reflect what he has done, heard, and learned from one special/comedy album to the next.

In *Bigger & Blacker*, Rock discussed a wide range of topics, from health care to women, racial issues to relationships. In one section, Rock criticized how little was being done about AIDS. He said the government was merely trying to figure out how people living with AIDS could get by—pushing the medicine rather than spending money to find a cure. He talked about race issues and what it meant to be white vs. black: "There ain't a white man in this room who'd change places with me. None of ya! And I'm rich! That's how good it is to be white.... When you white, the sky's the limit, and when you black, the limit's the sky."

Also at this time, Rock turned his attention to helping young black writers. When he was on *Saturday Night Live*, Rock wished there had been more black writers—he worked almost exclusively with white writers on the show. So now, realizing how few black comedy writers there were, Rock decided to develop a magazine called the *Illtop Journal* (modeled after *Harvard Lampoon*) at Howard University in Washington, D.C.

Rock hoped the magazine would offer insight and guidance to aspiring young comedy writers. Combining humor pieces written by college students with information about how to succeed in the business, the magazine urged writers to use writing to elevate the black social consciousness. Rock helped edit the first issues of the magazine. The university produced two issues, but with a lack of funds caused by a plummeting economy, the comedy magazine ceased publication. Rock still hopes to see it or a similar endeavor get off the ground, because he believes strongly in helping young black writers get started in a career field dominated by white people.

Rock was invited, again, to host the MTV Music Video Awards in 1999, this time broadcast from the Metropolitan Opera House in New York. "I may be the first black man to be on this stage without a mop," Rock cracked. Never one to shy away from aiming jokes at celebrities, Rock took jabs at many of the famous guests, including Jennifer Lopez and Ricky

Chris Rock was the host of the 1999 MTV Music Video Awards, which were held at the Metropolitan Opera House in New York. The show was the highest-rated entertainment program in cable history. Rock had hosted the Music Video Awards two years earlier as well.

Martin. The celebrities reacted with good humor toward Rock. The show became the highest-rated entertainment program in cable history.

Rock also made a return appearance to *Saturday Night Live* to perform the opening monologue for its twenty-fifth anniversary show on September 26, 1999. Although Rock had made a few appearances on *Saturday Night Live* since his departure in 1993, he was happy to return to the show and bring closure to his time there, because he had not left on the best of terms. The show paid tribute to Chris Farley, Rock's co-star and friend, as well as to other *Saturday Night Live* cast members who had died over the years.

In Rock's piece for the twenty-fifth anniversary, he made fun of everybody—the show, himself, and the cast:

> Welcome to the show. I'm out here because somebody had to do it. And I guess they thought I would be the best guy for it.… I look around this room, look at the star power. Look at the comedic genius. I'm looking at some of the most overrated people in the history of comedy! Some of the worst movies ever made were made by people in this room! Thank God we're gonna do what we all do best—television!

6

Chris Rock at Work

Even when Rock's career was going strong, he always maintained level-headedness and remained true to his father's work ethic. Rock knew that his success would not guarantee that he would be the "funniest man in America" forever. At any time, he felt, the industry could decide he was no longer "hot." To ensure that there were no gaps between paychecks, Rock put in his share of work hours. Occasionally that meant doing a project because it was offered, but Rock was lucky enough to have plenty of control over the parts he selected and to be able to write nearly all of his own material.

When Rock is on the clock, he prefers to work alone. He often puts on his iPod and listens to music while contemplating what to write. Rock frequently visits the Coffee Shop, located in New York City's Union Square. Here, he knows the employees and patrons will leave him alone. He sometimes feels bothered by the constant attention he receives—he misses the days when he could dine alone. Rock maintains a very small circle of friends. He sometimes hangs out with his fellow *Saturday Night Live* alum Adam Sandler. Like Rock, Sandler can relate to the problems that come with being famous and trying to live a relatively normal life.

Rock, however, does not lead a "normal" life. One day, Rock was returning home by plane from Los Angeles. When he stepped into the limo he had hired, he saw that the driver was a former classmate from James Madison High School. This guy had spit on Rock at school, but now he was very chatty and acted as if he and Rock were good friends. Rock made sure to give the driver an extra big tip upon leaving, hoping to make him wonder what Rock really thought of him. It stunned Rock to think that people could be so cruel to someone, then turn around and pretend to like them when they were rich and famous. He realized that when they were kids, the two were just playing roles: The driver was the white boy; Rock was the black boy in an all-white school. It was the white boy's job to beat up and insult the black boy. Rock tries to learn from moments like these; he tries to understand people better and to avoid holding grudges.

Rock doesn't have time for bitterness. He takes his routine seriously and, like his father before him, takes his work

IN HIS OWN WORDS...

Chris Rock has a strong work ethic, but he also places great importance on the *quality* of his work. In an interview with the *Guardian* newspaper of London, Rock said about his comedy:

I never wanted to churn it out. Comedians tend to work all the time. They never put it down like musicians who might make an album, then take three or four years off to recharge their batteries. Comedians tend to work straight through, and they get stale because of that. Even when I didn't have a lot of money I never ever did it unless I had something new to say.

seriously. And he believes in being a good person while he is working hard. At one show in Georgia, the crew was having trouble with the lights glaring off his shirt. The lighting people spent hours trying to correct the problem. After the rehearsal, Rock personally thanked each crew member for his or her time.

Rock is constantly on the lookout for new material. Some of it stems from everyday life—observations he makes while going about his daily activities. He also reads newspapers and magazines daily. When Rock thinks of an idea for his comedy routine, he calls home and records it on his answering machine or writes it down in his Palm Pilot. Later, he sifts out the material he wants to incorporate into his routine.

NEW PROJECTS

In September 2000, *Nurse Betty*, a film directed by Neil LaBute, premiered; Rock played a lead role opposite Morgan Freeman and Renée Zellweger. Working with Freeman, a veteran actor, allowed Rock to improve his acting skills. If Rock started to overact, Freeman would overact. This humorous, nonverbal cue helped Rock realize what he was doing and prompted him to tone down his performance. *Nurse Betty* received rave reviews and spent five weeks on the top-ten list.

In 2001, Rock appeared in *Pootie Tang*, directed by Louis C.K. and starring Lance Crouther. Rock was one of the film's producers, too. In the movie, Pootie Tang (played by Crouther) is a superhero idolized by women and children alike. He has a language all his own. The character was based on a skit that originated on *The Chris Rock Show*. In the movie, Rock played multiple roles. While the character of Pootie Tang may have worked in a short sketch, most critics agreed that there was not enough material to turn the idea into a movie.

Rock also was the executive producer and a writer (along with *Chris Rock Show* writers Ali LeRoi, Louis C.K., and Lance Crouther) of *Down to Earth*. This romantic comedy was a

Chris Rock costarred with Morgan Freeman (center) and Renée Zellweger (right) in the 2000 film *Nurse Betty*, directed by Neil LaBute. Freeman, a veteran performer, had a subtle way of showing Rock when he was overacting.

remake of a 1941 movie, *Here Comes Mr. Jordan*, which, in turn, was remade in 1978 as *Heaven Can Wait*. Rock starred as Lance, who mistakenly dies before his time and gets sent to heaven. Angels send him back to Earth, but the only body available is that of Charles Wellington, a white man just murdered by his wife. Wanda Sykes, another former *Chris Rock Show* writer, also starred in the movie. Rock wrote about the racial issues that stemmed from this comical situation.

Rock conferred with Bill Cosby during the making of *Down to Earth*. Rock had little experience as an executive producer of a film, and Cosby offered him advice. The movie collected poor reviews overall. Critics felt that the direction by Paul and Chris Weitz was weak and that the characters had no chance of developing.

Also in 2001, Rock provided the voices for characters in two movies. In *Artificial Intelligence: AI*, Rock gave voice to Comedian Mecha. *AI* starred Haley Joel Osment and Jude Law. The movie, directed and written by Steven Spielberg and released in June, was a box-office success and was well-received by critics. Rock also provided the voice for Osmosis Jones, a little white blood cell, in a PG-13–rated movie titled *Osmosis Jones*, which was released in August. The film, starring Bill Murray and directed by the Farrelly brothers, was part animation and part live action. Critics commended the animated sections of the movie but did not think that the live-action sections worked.

LANGUAGE ISSUES

Many critics have pointed out that what makes Rock stand out is his ability to take real-life moments that are not always funny and make people laugh about them. Some critics, however, are not laughing. Some feel that Rock uses too much profanity and that his messages and viewpoints get lost in the onslaught of bad language. Rock is not alone in his use of profanity. Many other comics use profanity in their routines—Richard Pryor did. Eddie Murphy, Whoopi Goldberg, Martin Lawrence, and Joe Torry all do. But there are also many successful comedians who never or very rarely swear—Bill Cosby is one. Sinbad, Mark Curry, and Jonathan Slocumb also keep their routines profanity-free.

When Rose Rock first heard her son perform, she had a hard time getting past his language. Chris never swore around his mother, so she was taken aback by the words she heard her son saying. She was upset. Even Cosby, Rock's childhood idol, criticized Rock's language. When Rock planned to use a reference to one of Cosby's comedy albums in *Bring the Pain*, Cosby would not allow it because he did not approve of Rock's language. Once Rose Rock, like so many of Chris Rock's fans, looked past the profanity, however, she saw that

Chris Rock and his mother, Rose Rock, attended the ceremony honoring the comedian with a star on the Hollywood Walk of Fame. When Rose Rock first heard of her son's stand-up act, she found it hard to get past the profanity he used. Over time, she came to hear the message delivered in his work.

his messages and insight were important and noteworthy. In a 1998 interview, Rose Rock said:

> At first, I didn't really listen to what he was saying because I got turned off with the language. And just in the past two years, I have really gotten the message. I see the message now. I'm really proud of what he is doing in those terms. I'm really proud of that. He would have never won an Emmy if it had not been for the message, and there is a great message there.

Some critics point out that Rock, like Richard Pryor before him, does not depend on profanity for shock value. While there are comics who need to swear to make their routines funny, Pryor would still be funny if the bad language was removed. Rock uses profanity to stress the point he is

From Hip Hop to Def Comedy Jam

The television program *Def Comedy Jam* was developed in the 1990s by an artistic visionary named Russell Simmons. Back in 1984, Simmons was the cofounder of a pioneering hip-hop record label called Def Jam. He helped start the careers of rappers Run-DMC, Public Enemy, LL Cool J, and the Beastie Boys. Through Def Jam, Simmons turned rap and hip-hop music into big business. Def Jam became just one part of Simmons's corporation, Rush Communications, which became the largest black-owned enterprise in the industry.

Another part of the business was the HBO television series *Def Comedy Jam*, which ran from 1992 to 1997. Critics called the Def Jam comedians "raw" and "outrageous." Martin Lawrence was the first host. Chris Rock was a frequent performer on the show. *Def Comedy Jam* provided a place predominantly for African Americans to showcase their work. Dave Chappelle, Cedric the Entertainer, D.L. Hughley, Bernie Mac, and Chris Tucker were just a few of these comedians. The program did for stand-up what rap did for music, bring black street life to the attention of an audience unfamiliar with it.

trying to convey. "My cursing is my punctuation," Rock said in one interview. Lorne Michaels, the executive producer of *Saturday Night Live*, told *Time* magazine, "At the time that Chris was coming up, the Def Comedy Jam style became the dominant African-American style of comedy. The shock there was in the language. But Chris was going with the shock of ideas."

In a 1999 interview with *Ebony* magazine, Rock described himself as a "hip-hop comedian." He said:

> I think a new breed of comedian is very hip-hop influenced. Like Chris Tucker or myself, guys who really get to the point right away, lots of jokes.... I think hip-hop gets into comedy that way, whereas a guy like Bill Cosby listens to a lot of jazz and he takes his sweet time to get to certain things. Hip-hop is immediate, and my comedy's immediate.

Rock does not dwell on the use of profanity in his routines. When he's onstage, he's not trying to be a role model for young children. He's trying to get laughs from adults. He's trying to put a spin on old ideas and get people to think. Maybe the language helps get the attention of some people who might not otherwise listen to Rock's ideas.

7

The Family Man

On September 11, 2001, the world changed. Terrorists, under orders from Osama bin Laden, attacked the World Trade Center in New York City and the Pentagon outside Washington, D.C. The terrorists hijacked four commercial U.S. airplanes. They crashed the first plane into the north tower of the World Trade Center and then crashed a second plane into the south tower. A third plane crashed into the Pentagon, and the fourth plane crashed in a Pennsylvania field after some of the passengers tried to stop the hijackers. The people aboard all four planes died instantly. Nearly 3,000 people died as a result of the destruction the airplanes caused. Businesses crumbled; people lost their jobs. Fires continued to burn at the World Trade Center site for 99 days after the attacks. The cost of cleanup totaled 600 million dollars. The events of September 11 would affect the lives of the American people for years to come.

As a result of the terrorist attacks, people in the United States and around the world were reminded just how precious life is. Chris Rock was no different. He and Malaak had been married for nearly five years. Soon after 9/11—knowing they wanted to create a family together—the couple decided to have a baby. Malaak Compton-Rock gave birth to their first daughter, Lola Simone, on June 28, 2002. Two years later, on May 22, the Rocks welcomed their second daughter, Zahra Savannah. Both girls were born in New York, where they lived for a few years in an ivy-covered carriage house in Brooklyn, not far from where Rock grew up. The family has recently moved to the suburbs of New Jersey.

Rock embraces fatherhood. Lola and Zahra bring him happiness each and every day. He takes his roles as a father and a husband seriously. He tries to parent by example. He believes that if you smoke, your child will smoke (so he chooses not to smoke); if you are responsible, your child will be responsible (so he aims to be responsible).

Rock wants to be the kind of parent who spends time with his children and is a constant presence in their lives. On a typical day, you might find the family watching *The Wiggles* or some other children's programming. Lola and Zahra have play dates and go to birthday parties—sometimes they play at big fancy houses, other times they play at small apartments. The four go on family vacations to places like Disney World in Orlando, Florida. It is important to the Rocks to keep their daughters' lives as normal as possible.

"I always say about my daughters, they save me from my miserable self. They take me out," Rock said in an interview. "You know, a comedian, you could live in your head a lot. And you're writing and you're doubting. But when I'm with my kids and my family, it's all about them."

The Rocks avoid the glitz and glamour that many entertainers pursue. Rock strives to spend money modestly. He uses the local barbershop when he needs a haircut and does not own a

Also enjoying the Hollywood Walk of Fame ceremony in 2003 with Chris Rock were Malaak Compton-Rock and their daughter, Lola Simone, who was nearly nine months old at the time. In 2004, the couple had a second daughter, Zahra Savannah. For the Rocks, it is important that their daughters' lives stay as normal as possible.

fleet of flashy cars or travel with an entourage. He takes care to save for his daughters' futures, as well as to ensure they have what they need in the present.

Whenever they get the chance, the Rocks like to spend evenings at home watching movies or listening to music. Unlike in his act, off-stage, Rock hardly ever raises his voice and swears only rarely. His manner is quiet and contemplative. Malaak Compton-Rock describes her husband as a soft romantic. He surprises her with getaways to places like Martha's Vineyard. He has a passion for music and painting. Rock says he goes into a record store nearly every day looking for music, and he

Safe Horizon and StyleWorks

Malaak Compton-Rock has dedicated much of her life to helping women succeed. She has used her celebrity status, as well as her husband's, to help promote nonprofit organizations. She is a member of the board of directors for Safe Horizon, an organization that supports victims of crime and abuse, their families, and their communities. Through more than 80 programs, Safe Horizon serves more than 350,000 New Yorkers annually. One such program is a hotline that women can call to get advice and help. Around 700 women from the New York City area take advantage of this hotline daily. The group also offers shelters for women who escape domestic violence, youth programs, and court-based programs.

Compton-Rock's work with StyleWorks, her nonprofit company, helps to promote a woman's sense of self, independence, and confidence. The organization assists women as they make the transition from welfare to work. She has helped hundreds of women in New York City turn their lives around by finding an inner sense of pride and an ability to meet life's challenges. Compton-Rock believes that by helping one individual woman, you are also helping that woman's family and extended community.

To find out more about StyleWorks, visit www.styleworks.org.

Chris Rock also supports Safe Horizon. On November 10, 2005, he did a video introduction for the organization's fall fundraiser. The fundraiser featured stand-up comics like Colin Quinn, Nick DiPaolo, Adam Ferrara, Lynne Koplitz, Sherrod Small, Wanda Sykes, and Rich Vos. The event raised about $400,000.

also enjoys art museums. Rock loves going to basketball games, especially when the Knicks are playing; he has season tickets and is often seen sitting courtside.

Malaak Compton-Rock, like her husband, maintains a busy career. She made a career change in late 1999. She ended her work at UNICEF to create and run a nonprofit company called StyleWorks. Based in Brooklyn, StyleWorks provides free services to women who enter the workforce after being on welfare. Compton-Rock oversees salons in New York that help the women with free makeovers, consultations, and mentorships. The motto of StyleWorks is "a fresh new look for a fresh new start."

Within three years, Compton-Rock's endeavors at Style-Works had really taken off. She appeared on *The Oprah Winfrey Show* to discuss her work. *Redbook* magazine featured her as a winner of the 2002 Mothers & Shakers Awards, honoring her accomplishments with StyleWorks. And *Crain's New York Business* magazine named Compton-Rock as one of the top 40 New York executives under the age of 40. Rock attends many of his wife's functions when he is able and supports her causes and projects. Compton-Rock hopes to expand the organization to help women returning to the workforce in other U.S. states.

MORE MOVIES

In 2002, the year Rock's first daughter was born, several movies featuring Rock were released. He was one of several comedians featured in a documentary called *Comedian*, directed by Christian Charles. The film followed Jerry Seinfeld's career for a year after the end of his sitcom. It chronicled Seinfeld's development of a new standup routine, from trying it out in small comedy clubs to putting on a national show. Paralleling Seinfeld's path, the movie also followed a lesser-known comedian named Orny Adams. Throughout the movie, viewers met other stand-up comics, including Chris Rock, Jay Leno, Robert Klein, Bill Cosby, and Colin Quinn. The movie received mainly positive reviews from the critics, most of whom agreed that it offered an insightful look at what it took to be a successful comedian. *Rolling Stone* magazine said *Comedian* was "an indispensable peek at the art and the agony of making people laugh."

Bad Company, an action comedy, also opened in 2002. In this movie, Rock played a hustler who has to fill in as a CIA agent for his brother, who was killed in the line of duty. Anthony Hopkins also starred in the film. The movie was shot in Prague, the capital of the Czech Republic, which Rock enjoyed very much. He was able to explore the city to find music stores in which to browse, one of his favorite pastimes. Originally, *Bad Company* was scheduled to be released in November 2001, but because of the September 11 attacks, the movie did not premiere until the following June. The subway scenes in the movie became some of the last scenes ever to be filmed at the World Trade Center. *Bad Company* received negative reviews from film critics, who often cited a poor script and weak performances from Hopkins and Rock.

DIRECTED BY CHRIS ROCK

On March 28, 2003, *Head of State*, which Rock wrote with Ali LeRoi, opened in theaters. Rock also produced, starred in, and made his directorial debut with this film. It came out just after Rock received a star on Hollywood's Walk of Fame. In *Head of State*, Rock played Mays Gilliam, a presidential candidate chosen to run after the original candidate is killed. Bernie Mac costars as Rock's brother, Mitch.

Rock first got the idea for the movie in 1984 when the Democrats, worried that they could not win against the Republican ticket of Ronald Reagan and George H.W. Bush, ran Geraldine Ferraro with Walter Mondale, creating a historic first with a woman vice presidential candidate. Rock used movies like *Dr. Strangelove* and *The Hudsucker Proxy* as influences for *Head of State*.

Chris Rock portrayed the presidential candidate Mays Gilliam in the 2003 film *Head of State*. Rock made his directorial debut with the film. He also cowrote it with Ali LeRoi. The film provided Rock with a platform to present his views on voting and elections in America.

Rock and LeRoi traveled to Washington D.C., where they stayed at the Four Seasons Hotel to work on the script. While in Washington, the writing team talked to several politicians, hoping to gain insight to aid their writing. Rock did not meet with either President George W. Bush or former President Bill Clinton. But he had attended some of the same functions as Clinton, and Rock has respect for him. Rock likes that Clinton is a "regular" person who doesn't try to be more than that. Rock duplicated that quality in the character he played. Collaborating with LeRoi led to plenty of laughter during the writing process, so Rock felt that the script would translate well onto the screen.

Rock used the movie to present his ideas about elections and voting in the United States. Because only half of Americans vote in an election in a good year, Rock wanted to explore what could happen if another 40 percent of the people voted. His character, Mays, and Mays's brother, Mitch, direct their campaign to that percentage of Americans who do not vote.

Rock found his role as director enjoyable. He had long admired director Woody Allen and was happy to be directing. "The movie is the director's movie," Rock said in an interview. "You can write the movie and star in the movie and have all of the 'control' you want. But if you don't direct the movie, then it's not your movie. It's half your movie at most."

He wanted the film to feel busy. Apparently it did, as some critics complimented Rock's ability to keep the movie moving at a strong pace (similar to what he does during his stand-up) while others found the pace to be choppy and inconsistent. Regardless of how the critics reviewed the film, Rock felt at home in the role of director. Having been the eldest in a family of seven children, he had regularly experienced being in charge of many people.

For the project, Rock worked foremost to create a comical movie, with some politics and self-awareness woven in. He wanted people to leave the theater after watching *Head of State* thinking about the issues that Mays the candidate addresses—such as our political system, welfare, and race.

8

Touring and the Oscars

Chris Rock's demanding schedule never let up. Along with making movies, he continued to make guest appearances on television programs, including *Real Time With Bill Maher, The Daily Show, Chappelle's Show,* and *The Graham Norton Effect.* He made numerous appearances on talk shows like *The Oprah Winfrey Show, Late Show With David Letterman, Late Night With Conan O'Brien, Ellen: The Ellen DeGeneres Show,* and *The Tonight Show With Jay Leno.*

On August 28, 2003, Rock was the host of MTV's 20th Anniversary Video Music Awards at Radio City Music Hall. Rock enjoyed being the host of the award show because he felt it kept him in touch with the "youth culture," now that he was nearing middle age. As the host of a show like the Video Music Awards, Rock does not like to use teleprompters. He prefers to keep his performance fresh and in the moment.

In his third round at the MTV awards, Rock received a warm welcome from the audience. Even though he again occasionally shocked the crowd with his intense lashings of celebrities in his monologue, critics gave Rock's hosting abilities a positive review. The 2003 show was another MTV success.

BLACK AMBITION

Over these last few years, Rock was busy with family life and movies. He became the father of two children, a role he truly loves. He wrote movies, starred in movies, directed a movie, and hosted an award show. As busy as he was, however, he had not done what he loved the most in his career—stand-up. Although he enjoyed his work in movies, Rock felt that stand-up was where his strengths were. He loved to perform for live audiences. He wanted to do another HBO special to showcase his stand-up. To prepare for the special, Rock did a club tour across the country, called *Black Ambition*.

When Rock was deciding what to include in his comedy routine, his main concern was to keep his observations relevant. He didn't want to look back and derive comedy from past events; he wanted to keep his commentary in the present to demonstrate his own growth since his last stand-up performances. In his early career, he talked about girlfriends and then later he talked about married life. So for his *Black Ambition* tour, he was ready to talk about fatherhood. Likewise, he wanted to include new commentary about current political and social issues.

IN HIS OWN WORDS...

Chris Rock doesn't shy away from talking about controversial subjects, including racism and politics. In one of his comedy routines, he says:

A black C student can't do [anything] with his life. A black C student can't be a manager at Burger King, meanwhile a white C student just happens to be the president of the United States.

One of the stops on Chris Rock's *Black Ambition* tour was at the Foxwoods Resort Casino in Connecticut. Rock used the tour to try out material and hone his act before taping his fourth HBO special, *Never Scared*. Some of his material covered his new role as a father.

Throughout his career, Rock had also been paying close attention to what other comedians were doing. He learned from watching others and thinking about why they did what they did. He enjoyed a wide range of comedians, including Chris Tucker, Dave Chappelle, Adam Sandler, Woody Allen, and Ellen DeGeneres. By watching and listening to other comics, Rock could constantly modify and freshen his own performance, his delivery, and his style.

Beginning in October 2003, Rock toured North America for five months, getting back in the swing of stand-up. He tried out his act to see what worked and what still needed work. He talked about being a father, health care, politics, gun control, women, relationships, abortion, gay marriage, and other issues. His tour received a favorable response—he performed to sold-out audiences in more than 65 cities across the United States and Canada.

NEVER SCARED

The *Black Ambition* tour led up to Rock's latest HBO comedy special (his fourth), *Never Scared*, performed in Washington, D.C., at DAR Constitution Hall, in April 2004. It was his first HBO special in more than four years. The network was excited to have him back. A few years earlier, Chris Albrecht, who was then president of original programming for HBO, told *Time* magazine, "HBO has been known for breaking top comedians, and Chris is the most important to come along in a long time. He's a guy who can get away with being honest in a way that few people can."

Never Scared premiered on HBO on April 17, 2004. The first visible difference between this comedy concert and his previous specials is Rock's growing maturity, which is apparent in his appearance: He wears a classy, neutral suit that reflects his age and shows sophistication.

Rock tells his audience right away that he's now a father. He goes on to talk about how a father's biggest responsibility to his daughter is to keep her off the pole—if your daughter becomes a stripper, you have failed as a father. Although the concert begins rather raunchily, Rock works up to the material he's known for: social commentaries about racism, relationships, and politics. He discusses the differences between "rich" and "wealthy": "Shaq is rich," he said, referring to NBA all-star Shaquille O'Neal. "The guy who signs his checks is wealthy."

Never Scared was nominated for two Emmys, and critics praised Rock's return to stand-up. Some critics felt the show did not quite live up to his previous comedy concerts, but most agreed that it was full of laughs and provided 90 minutes of fast-paced comedy without any pitfalls. The DVD also included a bonus feature of Rock's early work, *Chris Rock: Big Ass Jokes* from 1993.

HOST OF THE ACADEMY AWARDS

In October 2004, Chris Rock was named to host the 77th Annual Academy Awards. Between the announcement and the actual show, there was plenty of buzz about how Rock would do as the host: He was known for using profanity—would there need to be a time delay in case he swore? Rock was expected to be outrageous—but would he say something *too* over-the-top? Rock had some radical thoughts—would he be too cutting edge during the show?

Some people thought that his raw, honest humor would not lend itself to the Academy Awards. But the Academy hoped to make the show more appealing to younger audiences. Academy leaders defended their decision to hire Rock and sent him on a publicity tour to promote the show. On tour, Rock said he would not soften his material for the show, which further worried some people.

Rock hired ten writers, including Ali LeRoi, Lance Crouther, and John Macks. (Macks worked with Billy Crystal when he was the Oscars host.) With their help, Rock planned out the topics he hoped to cover and worked on his material. He wanted to keep the material geared toward what the audience at home would have been most likely to see—including movies that were not necessarily nominated for Academy Awards.

Not everyone liked Rock's Academy Awards performance at the Kodak Theatre in Hollywood on February 27, 2005; many

As the Academy Awards host, Chris Rock made a mock presentation about the accountants who tally up the results of the Oscar balloting. Some critics said Rock was too "mean-spirited" in his stint as Oscars host. Others found his performance funny.

critics found him to be "mean-spirited." Rock told the audience that filmmakers should wait for better talent instead of using small-time actors:

Clint Eastwood's a star, OK? Tobey Maguire's just a boy in tights. You want Tom Cruise and all you can get is Jude Law? Wait. You want Russell Crowe and all you can get is Colin Farrell? Wait. *Alexander* is not *Gladiator.* You want Denzel [Washington] and all you can get is me? Wait. Denzel's a fine actor. He woulda never made *Pootie Tang.*

Actor Sean Penn, along with others, thought Rock was disrespectful to Jude Law. When Penn took the stage later in the evening, he stood up for Law. Rock later defended his remarks as being merely jokes.

Rock also poked fun at President George W. Bush and award shows in general. Every year the Academy Awards tries to find ways to keep the show from running too long. In 2005, some awards were handed out in the aisles to save the winners the time of walking up to the stage. This led to Rock's joking that next year some Oscars would be presented in the parking lot, with winners taking advantage of a quickie drive-through lane. The show, overall, was uneventful compared with the attention it received beforehand. Rock's monologue was free of profanity and full of remarks highlighting the Academy and Hollywood stars. Simply stated, some people found the performance funny; others did not.

In the fall of 2005, Rock ruled out a return as Academy Awards host in 2006. His publicist told *The New York Times*: "He didn't want to do it in perpetuity. He'd like to do it again down the road."

9

The Big Screen
and the Small Screen

For Chris Rock, May 27, 2005, was a big day. Two of his movies were coming out on the same day: *The Longest Yard* was released by Paramount Pictures, and *Madagascar* was released by DreamWorks. In *The Longest Yard*, a remake of the 1974 prison football movie, Rock played "Caretaker," opposite Adam Sandler and Burt Reynolds. In the computer-animated children's film *Madagascar*, Rock was the voice of Marty the zebra. Each movie made over 100 million dollars.

DUAL RELEASE

The Longest Yard, directed by Peter Segal, is more of a comedy/action movie than the original. The 1974 film (also called *The Longest Yard*) placed more emphasis on the action. The plot is about a former football player named Paul Crewe who ends up in a Texas state penitentiary. One of the wardens wants Crewe to lead the prison-guard football team to a

Chris Rock reunited with Adam Sandler, his *Saturday Night Live* colleague, in the movie *The Longest Yard*. The prison football movie was their first film together. Costarring with them was Burt Reynolds (center). Sandler and Rock were nominated for a People's Choice Award for favorite on-screen match-up.

championship. Crewe agrees after recruiting a fellow convict team for the guards to practice against in preparation for the championship.

In the 1974 movie, Burt Reynolds played Paul Crewe. This time around, Reynolds played Coach Nate Scarborough, and Adam Sandler played Crewe. It had been more than a decade since Sandler and Rock last worked together on *Saturday Night Live*. This was their first movie together. In November 2005, Sandler and Rock were nominated for a People's Choice Award for favorite on-screen match-up for the film.

In *The Longest Yard*, Rock played a character called "Caretaker," who helped Coach Scarborough lead Crewe's team against the guards. Rock had many one-line jokes. Some critics felt that he was underused in the movie. Others enjoyed his role for what it was.

Rock had a good time working with the former professional football players and current professional wrestlers who appeared in the movie. He also enjoyed working with the rap star Nelly, who played Megget, a member of the convict team. Rock was familiar with working with other actors and comedians. Working with athletes and rappers, however—people who had different talents than he did—was new territory. He felt great admiration and respect for their abilities.

The Longest Yard was filmed at the New Mexico State Penitentiary. Cast members had fun making the movie; between shots, they played a lot of basketball. Most of the cast also attended football camp to prepare them for the movie. But Rock, who had no athletic scenes in the film, did not need to go to football camp. He later joked in an interview that he attended whistling camp to prepare for all the blowing of the whistle he would be doing as a coach.

A very different movie made for a very different audience, *Madagascar* was about four animals (a zebra, a lion, a hippo, and a giraffe) that get shipped from their home in a New York City zoo to Madagascar. The animated comedy did not preach high morals or have an obvious message, other than, perhaps, to stand by your friends.

Mostly, the movie is merely good-humored and warm-hearted fun. Rock's character, Marty (the zebra), celebrated his tenth birthday early in the movie. One of his memorable lines occurred during his birthday party when he said, "I'm

From left, David Schwimmer, Chris Rock, Jada Pinkett Smith, and Ben Stiller pose at the premiere of *Madagascar* in New York. They were holding puppets that represented their characters in the animated comedy. The actors have signed on to make a sequel to the film.

ten years old, and I don't even know if I'm black with white stripes or white with black stripes!" Lines like this brought laughs from the audience (including Rock's daughters, who were happy to finally get to see one of their father's movies).

The movie did not receive rave reviews—with critics often complaining about a thin plot—but it became DreamWorks's most successful original movie ever, after earning more than 500 million dollars at the worldwide box office. In the United States, it stayed among the top ten movies for eight weeks.

DreamWorks plans to make a sequel to *Madagascar*, expected to come out in 2008. The leading actors (Rock as the zebra, Ben Stiller as the lion, Jada Pinkett Smith as the hippo, and David Schwimmer as the giraffe) have all agreed to take part in the sequel.

THE ARISTOCRATS

The Aristocrats, released by ThinkFilm, opened in theaters on July 29, 2005. The unrated movie has no nudity, no sex, and no violence, yet it boasts of being "one of the most shocking movies you will ever see." Penn Jillette and Paul Provenza were the film's cocreators (Provenza was also the director). They filmed about 100 comedians—always telling the same joke—over a period of two years. The result is 89 minutes of extremely crude comedy. The movie was well-reviewed by critics.

The comedians who took part in the film, including George Carlin, Paul Reiser, Robin Williams, Sarah Silverman, and Drew Carey, tell their own versions of one particular joke. The joke has been around since the days of vaudeville; some call it the world's funniest joke, and others call it the world's worst joke. The joke begins, "A man walks into a talent agent's office with his family and says, 'Have I got an act for you!' The talent agent replies, 'So what do they do?' " From this point, comedians improvise to make the joke their own, generally trying to be as offensive and outrageous as possible. Every comedian tries to top other comedians in terms of shock value. Although the middle of the joke is always different, the beginning and the punch line remain the same. When the agent asks what the family calls itself, the man replies, "The Aristocrats."

Only two black comics are represented in the film: Rock and Whoopi Goldberg. In part, this is because some of the black comedians Provenza tried to recruit for the film were not available, but it is also because the joke is historically told by white comedians. Rock does not even tell the joke in the film. Provenza caught Rock backstage and captured Rock's explanation of why so few black comics tell the joke. Rock said that for years black comics had been able to be raunchier than white performers on stage because blacks had little chance of appearing on television or the radio. Because white performers had to tone down their act onstage, they developed this very raunchy joke to use privately. They used it to "warm up" backstage (telling their friends and fellow comedians) before going onstage and telling cleaner, "nicer" jokes to the public.

EVERYBODY HATES CHRIS

Rock's next endeavor was prime-time television—and he took it by storm. Rock is the executive producer and narrator of a UPN comedy called *Everybody Hates Chris*, which is filmed in Los Angeles, California. The title, a play on the hit show *Everybody Loves Raymond*, was thrown out by Chris Rock as a joke during a writing session. Everybody laughed, and the name stuck.

Rock originally presented the show to the Fox network, which turned him down. Dawn Ostroff, president of the UPN network, was excited to pick up the show. In turn, Rock was happy to have a network that believed in the show. The family sitcom, set in the early 1980s, is loosely based on Rock's childhood, growing up in Bedford-Stuyvesant. The show is funny and heartfelt at the same time. The humor stems from realistic family relations and emotions. The stories are character driven and smart. *Everybody Hates Chris* is set in flashback—Chris Rock (the narrator) is looking back at his life as a child. The actor who plays young Rock, 12-year-old Tyler James Williams, portrays Chris at age 13. Tyler began acting on *Sesame Street* at the age of four.

Although the show is based on Rock's own life, changes have been made. Rather than the real-life family of seven children, there are three. Like the real Rock, the Chris on the show is a black boy bused a long way to a nearly all-white school. But the fictionalized students at the white school do not represent any particular students from Rock's real school. Many of the plots have been changed some from Rock's life or are completely made up. Rock also points out that Tyler is a cuter kid than Rock at that age—Rock had crooked teeth.

On the show, Rock's father (also named Julius) is played by former National Football League player Terry Crews. (Crews played one of the convict football players in *The Longest Yard*.) The sitcom Julius is a combination of the late Julius Rock and John Amos (who played James Evans, Rock's favorite television-sitcom father on *Good Times*). The sitcom Julius, like the late Julius, is tight with money. He works two jobs to make ends meet. Crews views the style of the sitcom's parents as a return to parenting. The parents on *Everybody Hates Chris* are loving and supportive, but when they say "no," they mean it and follow through—and the children listen. Tichina Arnold plays Rock's mother, who is named Rochelle on the show. Rochelle is a strict disciplinarian with "100 recipes for whoopin' ass." She is determined to see her children grow up and make something

Loving Everybody Hates Chris

For the actors and others involved in *Everybody Hates Chris*, the opportunity to present a part of life rarely seen on television has been a welcome one. Here is a sampling of what they had to say:

"A hardworking black man on TV who's not a player or a goofball is rare. There are millions of Juliuses out there, but you never see them on TV," said Terry Crews, who plays Julius, in *Jet* magazine.

"I was attracted to Rochelle because of the strength of her character. And the fact that we haven't seen a black family in a long time portrayed the way we're portrayed—with love, strength and honesty. A lot of people were able to identify with it in addition to the fact that it's not just for black people. The wonderful thing is that Italian women and Jewish women walk up to me all the time saying, 'Oh my God, my mom says the same things to me.' It crosses a lot of cultural barriers, and a lot of people are able to get it.... To portray a black family on television that all cultures can relate to is very rewarding," said Tichina Arnold, who plays Rochelle, in *Jet* magazine.

"Watching other shows, children talk back to parents. In real life it wouldn't get that far, especially in African-American families. I was of themselves. Arnold is pleased to be a part of the show and believes that television lacked a program like *Everybody Hates Chris*, which emphasizes family values and old-fashioned parenting. "Television needs this show right now," Arnold said. "It's heartfelt."

The two other siblings on the show have different names from any of Rock's real-life siblings. The sitcom brother's name is Drew, played by Tequan Richmond, and the sitcom sister's name is Tanya, played by Imani Hakim. Drew is younger than his brother, Chris, but is taller and more at ease around girls. Tanya is the baby of the family who always gets her way.

Rock and his longtime collaborator and friend, Ali LeRoi (who is also an executive producer), came up with the premise for the show and wrote the premiere episode. The show uses a

hoping it would be like this because that never happens. Kids don't talk back to parents and get away with it and get a hug," said Tyler James Williams, who plays Chris, in *Jet* magazine.

"Guys love their wives. It does happen. It's not all Al Bundy," said Crews in *The Atlanta Journal-Constitution*.

"Here's the thing that separates this from every other show of this type that you've seen: You know how the story ends.... We know that [the young Chris character] became Chris Rock, this acerbic, wry, and caustic comedian. What turned him into this guy? Where did he get the point of view that informs those observations? What was it about his mother and father and this difficult landscape, these experiences, that shaped him? For one thing he had a strong nuclear family, which is something that set him apart from the rest of his crowd. Does that mean everything in the show is using his particular experiences? Does he really have a hundred stories that are interesting enough for a series? Well, there might be 30. So we'll be using some poetic license. We're gonna fill in the gaps," said co-creator Ali LeRoi in *The New York Times*.

team of writers to create the scripts. LeRoi manages the writers and crew and calls the shots on the set. Rock and LeRoi have a unique ability to combine three kinds of comedy into the show and make them all work: realistic comedy (humorous incidents that happen in everyday life); wit and insight (Rock's narration voice-over heard off and on throughout the show); and the absurd (fantasy and dream sequences). In an interview with *The Cincinnati Post*, LeRoi said, "We're just taking real situations as much as we can and trying to find the comedy, as opposed to trying to manufacture comedy out of artifice."

When critics and advertisers previewed the show in May, they were impressed. The show generated much hype and interest. UPN did what it could to promote its new show, spending around 13 million dollars in marketing, which is more than twice what it normally spends on new sitcoms.

The season opened on September 22, 2005. *Everybody Hates Chris* was shown during one of the hottest time slots on primetime: on Thursday night against *Survivor: Guatemala, Joey*, and *Alias*. Nonetheless, *Everybody Hates Chris* was a big hit. UPN had its highest rating ever for a sitcom; 7.8 million viewers tuned in to watch the series premiere. More people watched *Everybody Hates Chris* that night than watched *Joey*. Even though the total number of viewers dropped 22 percent from its premiere to the second week, the show has given UPN a solid spot in the competitive Thursday-night lineup.

Everybody Hates Chris appeals to all ages. The show has been compared to *The Cosby Show* and *The Wonder Years*. Critics liked it because it was nice (the characters love and respect one another) without being preachy or forced. Critics called it one of the best sitcoms to depict what it is like to grow up poor since *Roseanne*.

After a sensational premiere, UPN agreed to 9 additional episodes of the show from its initial order of 13 episodes. That ensured *Everybody Hates Chris* a full season of 22 episodes. In addition, the Parents Television Council placed the show on its

Tichina Arnold, who plays the mother, Rochelle, on *Everybody Hates Chris*, accepts the award for best new series at the Seventh Annual Family Television Awards in Beverly Hills, California. Tyler James Williams, who plays Chris on the show, holds the award. With them on stage are (from left) Terry Crews (who plays the father, Julius), Vincent Martella (Greg), executive producer Ali LeRoi, Imani Hakim (Tanya), and Tequan Richmond (Drew).

annual list of the best prime-time shows for family viewing. Rock enjoys his work on his new sitcom. He spends most of his time with the director, quietly watching the show's progress and offering his input when needed.

"I just wanted to show a normal happy family," Rock said in an interview with *Jet* magazine. "There aren't a lot of poor people on TV, and it's kind of interesting to see a poor family trying to make it."

10

Philanthropy With a Smile

On August 25, 2005, Hurricane Katrina hit the east coast of Florida, just north of Miami. Four days later, the eye of the hurricane hit Louisiana early in the morning. A few hours later, much of the levee system in New Orleans failed, causing Lake Pontchartrain and the Mississippi River to flood nearly all of New Orleans. The hurricane damaged coastal regions of Louisiana as well as Mississippi and Alabama. More than 1,000 people died as a result of the hurricane. It caused around 200 billion dollars in damage. More than one million people were displaced; thousands were bused to neighboring states.

HURRICANE RELIEF

Chris Rock wanted to help. He joined Oprah Winfrey's Angel Network team to help hurricane survivors. The team spent time with evacuees at the Benita House of Hope in Houston, Texas, offering assistance and support. More than 100 displaced Louisiana residents moved into the house after Katrina hit. Rock went back three weeks later with his wife, Malaak. Rock said he thought the time he spent in Texas would have an effect on him for the rest of his life. He was reminded, as he was after 9/11, of the preciousness of life and the importance of family.

Rock also participated in a celebrity event called *Shelter From the Storm: A Concert for the Gulf Coast*, seen and heard on September 9, to aid victims of Katrina. The six biggest broadcast networks (ABC, CBS, NBC, Fox, UPN, and WB), other cable networks, radio stations, and the Internet carried the hour-long telethon, allowing people across the world to witness the program. Viewers and listeners were urged to contribute to the American Red Cross and/or the Salvation Army. Along with Rock, some of the participating celebrities included actors Morgan Freeman, Jack Nicholson, Jennifer Aniston, and Julia Roberts; comedians Ellen DeGeneres and Ray Romano; and musical acts U2, Kanye West, and Sheryl Crow.

Rock's contribution to the show received some attention in the media. His comment "George Bush hates midgets" was said very quietly into the microphone just before he began his actual tele-prompted monologue, which sought the help of viewers to aid hurricane survivors. Rock's midget comment was jokingly said in reference to rapper Kanye West's remark a week earlier (on an NBC hurricane relief fund-raiser) that George Bush doesn't care about black people.

Shelter From the Storm raised about 30 million dollars for the Katrina relief efforts of the American Red Cross and the Salvation Army. The money was used to provide food, shelter, and comfort to the hurricane survivors.

Rock also performed for a telethon on the Black Entertainment Television (BET) network that appeared the same night as *Shelter From the Storm*. The two-part, four-hour telethon was held in partnership with BET, the National Urban League, and the American Red Cross. Numerous performers,

Chris Rock took part in the *ReAct Now: Music and Relief* television special, an effort by MTV, VH1, and CMT to raise money for victims of Hurricane Katrina. It was one of several benefits Rock participated in to aid those affected by Katrina.

including jazz artist Wynton Marsalis, rapper Master P, and visionary Russell Simmons, appeared on the telethon. At the start of his performance, Rock joked: "Don't forget—George Bush hates albinos." The following day, September 10, Rock participated in the *ReAct Now: Music and Relief* television special to aid the hurricane victims.

Rock continued his relief efforts by serving as an honorary committee member of the fourth annual Robert S. Browne Philanthropist With a Vision Awards in October 2005. The committee members, as a part of The Twenty-First Century Foundation, honored Tavis Smiley, Wilbert Tatum, Spencer Means, and JoAnn Price for their philanthropic leadership. Proceeds from the awards dinner went to the Hurricane

Katrina Recovery Fund, the Black Men and Boys Initiative, and other resources for social justice initiatives in the black community.

MAYBE LAUGHTER IS THE BEST MEDICINE

What is in the future for Chris Rock? More comedy. More laughs. More living. Due to open in 2006 are the comedy films *Sick Day* and *The Gilmores of Beverly Hills.* An untitled film in which Rock will star with one of his first idols, Eddie Murphy, is slated to come out in 2007.

Comedy will always remain Rock's passion. He gives audiences a new way of looking at topics that are sometimes uncomfortable and often controversial. His comedy is street-smart and honest. He's not afraid to offend. He's not afraid to

Wit

Chris Rock's humor is smart and bold. He has mastered wit. Here is what other famous people have noted about the importance of wit:

"Instead of working for the survival of the fittest, we should be working for the survival of the wittiest—then we can all die laughing." —Lily Tomlin

"Wit is the sudden marriage of ideas which, before their union, were not perceived to have any relation." —Mark Twain

"There's a helluva distance between wisecracking and wit. Wit has truth in it; wisecracking is simply calisthenics with words."—Dorothy Parker

"You can pretend to be serious; you can't pretend to be witty."—Sacha Guitry, French actor and playwright

Rock's witty observations about life help to define his comedy. He is able to note truths and irony in situations that cause audiences to cry and laugh at the same time. His humor has a depth and meaning that is found in only a handful of comedic greats.

look audience members straight in the eye. He makes fun of white people and black people, men and women, fat people and skinny people, the rich and the poor.

Rock suffered deeply during his school days, and perhaps that suffering led to his take on life today. Maybe if Rock had gone to a public school in Bed-Stuy, he would not have so ingeniously developed his humor. Rock's stand-up offers listeners a new way of looking at issues—sometimes they will agree with him, sometimes not. Either way, Rock sheds light on ideas that get audiences thinking.

As young comedians begin their careers, they will study the greats before them to figure out what made those comedians rise above the rest. Chris Rock will be one of the comedians they study. *Entertainment Weekly* and *Time* magazine have both hailed Rock as "the funniest man in America." Rock knows that tomorrow magazines could start naming another comedian as the funniest man in America; he does not take the title too seriously.

Rock takes great interest in the world around him, noting the absurdities, the quirks, and the catch-22s. He incorporates those ideas into a routine—a stand-up act, a movie, or an HBO special—to share with the world. When Rock strides across the stage and shouts out his smart satire, the response

IN HIS OWN WORDS...

On *The Chris Rock Show,* Rock gave the following advice to aspiring young comics:

> If you don't live in New York or L.A., move. That would be my first piece of advice. If you want to make cars, you live in Detroit. Wanna be in show business, you live in New York or L.A.... You got to write. Just got to find your own voice and study. You got to really be on top of what everybody's doing and what everybody did before you.

Chris Rock appeared in the pressroom at the 37th Annual NAACP Image Awards, held on February 25, 2006, in Los Angeles. *Everybody Hates Chris* won the award for outstanding comedy series.

is immediate—he hears the laughs and applause and he knows he is on target. He knows that he has found that angle to one of life's doldrums, norms, or oddities, and has discovered the humor in it. Chris Rock does not care about the Emmys or the glamour that fame brings. He is all about performing.

More than anything, Chris Rock wants to make audiences laugh—because for him, comedy is what it's all about.

FILMS

Beverly Hills Cop II (1987)

I'm Gonna Git You Sucka (1988)

New Jack City (1991)

Boomerang (1992)

CB4 (1993)—also writer

The Immortals (1995)

Panther (1995)

Sgt. Bilko (1996)

Beverly Hills Ninja (1997)

Doctor Dolittle (1998)

Lethal Weapon 4 (1998)

Torrance Rises (1999)

Dogma (1999)

Nurse Betty (2000)

Down to Earth (2001)—also writer

Artificial Intelligence: AI (2001)

Pootie Tang (2001)

Osmosis Jones (2001)

Jay and Silent Bob Strike Back (2001)

Bad Company (2002)

Comedian (2002)

Head of State (2003)—also writer and director

The Aristocrats (2005)

The Longest Yard (2005)

Madagascar (2005)

TELEVISION SHOWS/VIDEOS

Uptown Comedy Express (1987)

Comedy's Dirtiest Dozen (1988)

Who Is Chris Rock? (1989)

Saturday Night Live (1990–1993)

Chris Rock: Big Ass Jokes (1993)

In Living Color (1993–1994)

Politically Incorrect (1996)

Chris Rock: Bring the Pain (1996)

The Chris Rock Show (1997–2000)

Chris Rock: Bigger & Blacker (1999)

Chris Rock: Never Scared (2004)

Everybody Hates Chris (2005–)

COMEDY ALBUMS

Born Suspect (1992)

Roll With the New (1997)

Bigger & Blacker (1999)

Never Scared (2004)

PRODUCER

CB4 (coproducer)

Chris Rock: Bring the Pain (executive producer)

The Chris Rock Show (executive producer)

The Hughleys (1998–2002) (executive producer)

Chris Rock: Bigger & Blacker (executive producer)

Down to Earth (executive producer)

Pootie Tang (producer)

Head of State (producer)

Chris Rock: Never Scared (executive producer)

Everybody Hates Chris (executive producer)

AWARDS

1994   CableACE Award (best stand-up comedy special) for *Chris Rock: Big Ass Jokes*

1997   CableACE Awards (best entertainment host and best variety special/series) for *The Chris Rock Show*; Emmy Awards (outstanding variety, music, or comedy special and outstanding writing for variety or music program) for *Bring the Pain*; Grammy Award (best spoken comedy album) for *Roll With the New*

1999   Blockbuster Entertainment Award (favorite supporting actor) for *Lethal Weapon 4*; Grammy Award (best spoken comedy album) for *Bigger & Blacker*; Emmy Award (outstanding writing for a variety or music program) for *The Chris Rock Show*

2000   American Comedy Award for *Bigger & Blacker*

2001   ShoWest Award for Comedy Star of the Year; National Association of Minorities in Communications Vision Awards (best variety program) for *The Chris Rock Show*

2004   Chosen number 5 among Comedy Central's 100 Greatest Stand-Ups of All Time

2006   NAACP Image Award for *Everybody Hates Chris* for outstanding comedy series

1965 Born on February 7 in Georgetown, South Carolina

1971 Moves with family to Brooklyn, New York, first to Crown Heights and then to Bedford-Stuyvesant

1973–1983 Is bused from Bedford-Stuyvesant to Bensonhurst to attend elementary school and high school

1983 Drops out of high school; earns G.E.D.; takes odd jobs

1985 Begins performing at comedy clubs around New York City

1986 Eddie Murphy spots Rock at the Comic Strip

1989 Rock's father, Julius, dies from complications after a ruptured ulcer

1990 Joins the cast of *Saturday Night Live*

1991 Releases his first comedy album, *Born Suspect*

1992 His friend and mentor Sam Kinison dies

1993 Leaves *Saturday Night Live*; meets Malaak Compton; they begin to date; makes his first HBO special, *Chris Rock: Big Ass Jokes*

1996 Makes a commitment to improve his comedy; makes his second HBO special, *Chris Rock: Bring the Pain*; marries Malaak Compton in Oxon Hill, Maryland

1997 Makes another comedy album, *Roll With the New*; writes and stars in *The Chris Rock Show*, on HBO; his book, *Rock This!*, is published; Chris Farley, his friend and former *Saturday Night Live* colleague, dies of a cocaine and heroin overdose

1999 Makes his third HBO special, *Bigger & Blacker*

2002 Daughter Lola Simone is born

2003 *Head of State*, the first movie directed by Rock, is released

2004 Second daughter, Zahra Savannah, is born; makes his fourth HBO special, *Never Scared*

2005 Is host of the 77th Annual Academy Awards ceremony; takes part in aiding survivors of Hurricane Katrina; creates a prime-time television show, *Everybody Hates Chris*, based on his own childhood growing up in Bedford-Stuyvesant

Miller, James A. and Tom Shales. *Live From New York: An Uncensored History of Saturday Night Live, As Told By Its Stars, Writers and Guests.* New York: Back Bay Books, 2003.

Rock, Chris and David Rensin. *Rock This!,* New York: Hyperion, 1997.

WEBSITES

Chris Rock
www.chrisrock.com

Comedy Central's entry on Chris Rock
www.comedycentral.com/comedians/browse/r/chris_rock.jhtml

Everybody Hates Chris
www.upn.com/shows/everybody_hates_chris/

Everybody Hates Chris Online
www.everybodyhateschris.org

The Internet Movie Database, "Chris Rock"
www.imdb.com/name/nm0001674/

Index

Picture Credits

page:

3: Associated Press, AP
6: LC-U9-2906-15,
   Library of Congress
16: Time Life Pictures/
   Getty Images
18: Time Life Pictures/
   Getty Images
23: Associated Press, AP
24: Warner Bros./Photofest
26: Associated Press, AP
29: Universal/Photofest
35: Getty Images
39: Getty Images

45: Getty Images
50: Gramercy Pictures/Photofest
52: Getty Images
57: Associated Press, AP
61: DreamWorks/Photofest
65: Associated Press, AP
68: Associated Press, AP
71: Paramount Pictures/
   Photofest
73: Associated Press, AP
79: Associated Press, AP
82: Associated Press, AP
85: Associated Press, AP

Cover: Getty Images

Anne M. Todd lives in Prior Lake, Minnesota, with her husband, Sean, and three sons, Spencer, William, and Henry. She received a Bachelor of Arts degree in English and American Indian Studies from the University of Minnesota. She has written more than a dozen nonfiction children's books, including biographies on world political leaders and American Indians, as well as several accounts of American history.